Smith Wigglesworth

JOY UNSPEAKABLE AND FULL OF GLORY

Righteousness Peace and JOY

Dr Michael H Yeager

Copyright © 2021 Dr. Michael H Yeager

All rights reserved.

ISBN: 9798464003309
Imprint: Independently published

DEDICATION

These Sermons, Teachings and Experiences from **Smith Wigglesworth** have been **MODERNIZED** for those who truly hunger and thirst after all that **God** has made available through the life, ministry, sufferings, death and resurrection of **Jesus Christ**. My prayer is that not only will your life be touched by these **divine Truths**, but you yourself will truly step in to that realm where all things are possible .**God** is not a respecter of people, what he did for **Smith Wigglesworth**, he desires to do for you and me. May you experience **Wonderful** transformation and divine healing.

These true stories and Sermons have been modernized in order to make them more understandable and descriptive in our modern vernacular. All of the Sermons have been compiled from many different articles, books, stories, sermons, and writings of Smith Wigglesworth. Some of these are laso taken from the internet! There are acknowledgments throughout this book to give credit to those who recorded the stories, and wrote them down for the increase and benefit of our personal faith. Jesus Christ is the same yesterday today and forever. What he did for these people he will do for you and me!

CONTENTS

Acknowledgments	i
Chapter One	1
Chapter Two	19
Chapter Three	29
Chapter Four	44
Chapter Five	59
Chapter Six	75
Chapter Seven	91
Chapter Eight	109
Chapter Nine	126
Chapter Ten	142

Smith Wigglesworth - JOY Unspeakable and Full of Glory

EXHORTATION

Smith Wigglesworth: This Is the Place Where God Will Show up!

You must come to a place of ashes, a place of helplessness, a place of wholehearted surrender where you do not refer to yourself. You have no justification of your own in regard to anything. You are prepared to be slandered, to be despised by everybody. But because of His personality in you, He reserves you for Himself because you are godly, and He sets you on high because you have known His name (Ps. 91:14). He causes you to be the fruit of His loins and to bring forth His glory so that you will no longer rest in yourself. Your confidence will be in God. Ah, it is lovely. "The Lord is the Spirit; and where the Spirit of the Lord is, there is liberty" (2 Cor. 3:17).

Born June 10th, 1859
Died March 4th, 1947

*Notice: There will be some repetition in this book. Please do not be offended by this fact.

Smith Wigglesworth, often referred to as 'the Apostle of Faith,' was one of the early pioneers of the Pentecostal revival that occurred a century ago.

Without human refinement and education he was able to tap into the infinite resources of God to bring divine grace to multitudes.

Thousands came to Christian faith in his meetings, hundreds were healed of serious illnesses and diseases as supernatural signs followed his ministry.

A deep intimacy with his heavenly Father and an unquestioning faith in God's Word brought spectacular results and provided an example for all true believers of the Gospel.

May this site stir your faith and deepen your vision for the glory of God in our generation.

CHAPTER ONE
REJOICING THE HEART

1 Peter 1:7 that the trial of your faith, being much more precious than of gold that perisheth, though it be tried with fire, might be found unto praise and honour and glory at the appearing of Jesus Christ: 8 whom having not seen, ye love; in whom, though now ye see him not, yet believing, ye Rejoice with JOY unspeakable and full of glory: 9 receiving the end of your faith, even the salvation of your souls.

"No-one can live after seeing God; and God wants us ALL to see Him so that we shall joyfully cease to be-- and that HE may become our life."

"Real faith has perfect peace and JOY, and a shout at any time. It always sees the victory."

Let heaven come in; let the Holy Ghost take possession of you, and when He comes into your body you will find out that is the keynote of the Spirit of JOY and the Spirit of rapture, and if you will allow the Holy Ghost to have full control you will find you are living in the Spirit, and you will find out that the opportunities will be God's opportunities, and there is a difference between God's opportunities and ours. You will find you have come to the right place at the right time, and you will speak the right word at the right time and in the right place, and you will not go a warfare at your own charge.

"No-one can live after seeing God; and God wants us ALL to see Him so that we shall joyfully cease to be-- and that HE may become our life."

God rejoices when we manifest a faith that holds Him to His word.

Faith is the audacity that rejoices in the fact that God cannot break His own Word!

Smith Wigglesworth - **JOY Unspeakable and Full of Glory**

Smith Wigglesworth Danced Every Morning before the Lord

It is said about Smith Wigglesworth that he use to get up every morning. He danced before the **Lord** for 10 minutes as a dance of Thanksgiving. He just could not help himself. It was not spiritual aerobics that he did to impress people. It simply was an expression of his **Gratitude** and his devotion for what **Jesus Christ** meant to him and had done for him. Every night we should go to sleep with a **Thankful** heart and wake up with a **Thankful** heart for our salvation.

"I don't ever ask Smith Wigglesworth how he feels!" I jump out of bed! I dance before the Lord for at least 10 to 12 minutes – high speed dancing. I jump up and down and run around my room telling God how great he is, how Wonderful He is, how Glad I am to be associated with Him and to be His child."

WIGGLESWORTH TOLD PEOPLE TO LEAVE

This is a story that I heard about Smith Wigglesworth. I cannot guarantee that is true.

Smith Wigglesworth was very forceful when it came to expressing your love, **Gratitude** and **Appreciation** to **Jesus Christ**. Some might be critical of his attitude, but I really do not know anybody personally that has ever walked in the same place he did.

Doc Yeager: Yes, I have had amazing miracles in many areas of my life, but none as consistent and as many as Smith had.

The story says that one time he was ministering at a church. When Smith got up to speak, he mentioned the Scriptures that talks about coming into **God**'s presence with **praise** and thanksgiving.

Psalm 100:4 Enter into his gates with thanksgiving, and into his courts with praise: be Thankful unto him, and bless his name.

After Smith made this statement, he asked the congregation a question: **"Well, who came in properly?"**. With not one response, he asked everybody to leave the sanctuary! Once everyone was out, he told them not to re-enter until they found something to be **Grateful** about, something to be **Thankful** about, something worthy of shouting the praises of **God** for! He told them: **come back in here with a shout or appraise when you are ready**.

All the congregation got up and walked out including the preacher. One by one, each person re-entered with a changed heart shouting and praising **God**! The meeting WHENT THROUGH THE ROOF!

I think most ministers today if they did this in the majority of the churches, even those who claim to be spiritual would be highly offended. Most likely they would leave with a bad attitude and never come back.

Smith Wigglesworth - JOY Unspeakable and Full of Glory

This is how far the modern day church has backslid from meekness and humility. Most of them are out of the will of **God** and proud of it. People who confess to know **Jesus** do not want to be told what to do even if it is **God** himself telling us by his Scriptures.

Smith would wake up every morning with his heart filled with deep **Appreciation** and **JOY**. With that type of attitude, you will never wake up on the wrong side of the bed. I wish I could say that I was the same. One morning I woke up and I decided to try it. I think I danced for five minutes, and I was tuckered out. How could Smith dance every morning through his 50s, 60s, 70s, and even 80s and still do this? I believe the answer is the **JOY** of the **Lord**.

You see the **JOY** of the **Lord** is our strength. **Jesus** because of the **JOY** that was set before him endured the cross, despising the shame. But now he is seated at the right hand of the Heavenly **Father**.

SMITH WIGGLESWORTHS TEACHING

I like what Smith Wigglesworth said who was mightily used of **God**: **Smith Wigglesworth:** This Is The Place Where **God** Will Show up!

You must come to a place of ashes, a place of helplessness, a place of wholehearted surrender where you do not refer to yourself. You have no justification of your own in regard to anything. You are prepared to be slandered, to be despised by everybody.

But because of His personality in you, He reserves you for Himself because you are godly, and He sets you on high because you have known His name (Ps. 91:14). He causes you to be the fruit of His loins and to bring forth His glory so that you will no longer rest in yourself.

Your confidence will be of **God**. Ah, it is lovely. "The **Lord** is the **Spirit**; and where the **Spirit** of the **Lord** is, there is liberty" (2 Cor. 3:17). "Before **God** could bring me to a place of Authority He had broken me a thousand times." ***Born June 10th, 1859 - Died March 4th, 1947***

Smith - My Bible is my heavenly bank. I find everything I want in it.

Beware of Covetousness

There is one thing I am very **Grateful** to the **Lord** for, and that is that He has given me grace not to have a desire for money. The love of money is a great hindrance to many; and many a man is crippled in his ministry because he lets his heart to run after financial matters.

Smith Wigglesworth - JOY Unspeakable and Full of Glory

I was walking out one day when I met a godly man who lived opposite of my house, and he said, "My wife and I have been talking together about selling our house and we feel constrained to sell it to you." As we talked together, he persuaded me to buy his place, and before we said good-by, I told him that I would take it. We always make big mistakes when we are in a hurry. I told my wife what I had promised, and she said, "How will you manage it?"

I told her that I had managed things so far, but I did not know how I was going to keep this commitment. I somehow knew that I was out of **God**'s divine will. But when a fellow gets out of Gods will, it seems that the last person he goes to is **God** himself. I was relying on an architect to help me, but that scheme fell through. I turned to my relations, and I certainly ended up with mud on my face as one after another turned me down. I tried my friends and managed no better. My wife said to me, "Thou hast never been to **God** Yet." What could I do?

I have a certain place in our house where I go to pray. I have been there more times then I can count through the years. As I went, I said, "**Lord**, if you will get me out of this mess I got myself into, I will never allow myself to be so foolish again." As I waited on the **Lord**, He just gave me one word. It seemed a ridiculous thing, but it was the wisest counsel. There is divine wisdom in every word **God** speaks.

I came down to my wife, saying, "What do you think? The **Lord** has told me to go to Brother Webster." I said, "It seems very ridiculous, for he is one of the poorest men I know." He was the poorest man I knew, but he was also the richest man I knew, for he knew **God**. He was a man who found his contentment in **God**, and not the things of this world! My wife said, "Do What **God** says, and **God** will deliver you."

I went off at once to see him. As he greeted me, he said: "Smith, what brings you so early?" I answered, "The word of **God**." I said to him, "About three weeks ago I promised to buy a house from a man, and I am short 100 pounds. (In 1930 one pound was equivalent to about $200 USA dollars in today's market. This means Smith was about $20,000.00 dollars.) I have tried to get this money, but somehow I seem to have missed **God** in this endeavor." "How is it," he asked, "that you have come to me only now?" I answered, "Because I went to the **Lord** about it only last night."

"Well," he said, "it is a strange thing; three weeks ago, I had 100 pounds. For years I have been putting money into a co-operative system and three weeks ago I had to go and draw 100 pounds out. I hid it under the mattress.

Come with me and you shall have it. Take it. I hope it will bring as great a blessing to you as it has been a trouble to me." I had my word from **God**, and all my troubles were ended. This lesson has been multiplied in a hundred ways since that time.

If I had been walking along filled with the **Holy Ghost**, I would not have bought that house and would not have had all that pressure. If I had been in the **Spirit** material things would not have interested me! I believe the **Lord** wants to deliver us from things of earth. But I am ever **Grateful** for that word from **God**.

PS: Smith lived in the same house until he died! Even though he became one of the most successful ministers of his day, he never let it pull him into a lavish life style!

SMITH WIGGLESWORTH ATTITUDE TOWARDS CALVINISM (OSAS)

God says to us, "In patience possess thy soul." How beautiful! There have been in England great churches which believed once saved always saved. I thank **God** that they are all disappearing. You will find if you go to England those hardheaded people that used to hold on to these things are almost gone. Why? Because they went on to say whatever you did, if you were elect, you were right. That is so wrong.

The elect of **God** is those that keep pressing forward. The elect of **God** cannot hold still. They are always on the move. Every person that has a knowledge of the elect of **God** realizes it is important that he continues to press forward. He cannot endure sin nor darkness nor things done in the shadows. The elect is so in earnest to be right for **God** that he burns every bridge behind him.

"Knowing this, that first there shall be a falling away"

Knowing this, that first **God** shall bring into His treasury the realities of the truth and put them side by side — the false, and the true, those that can be shaken in mind, and those that cannot be shaken in mind. **God** requires us to be so built upon the foundation of truth that we cannot be shaken in our mind, it doesn't matter what comes.

I WAS ALONE WITH GOD

Then **God** gave me a revelation. Oh, it was **Wonderful**! He showed me an empty cross and **Jesus** glorified. I do thank **God** that the cross is empty, that **Christ** is no more on the cross. It was there that He bore the curse, for it is written, "Cursed is everyone that hangeth on a tree." He became sin for us that we might be made the righteousness of **God** in Him, and now, there He is in the glory.

Then I saw that **God** had purified me. It seemed that **God** gave me a new vision, and I saw a perfect being within me with mouth open, saying, "Clean l Clean! Clean!" When I began to repeat it I found myself speaking in other tongues. The **JOY** was so great that when I came to utter it my tongue failed, and I began to **worship God** in other tongues as the **Spirit** gave me utterance.

It was all as beautiful and peaceful as when **Jesus** said, "Peace, be still!" and the tranquility of that moment and the **JOY** surpassed anything I had ever known up to that moment. But, **Hallellujah** l these days have grown with greater, mightier, more **Wonderful** divine manifestations and power. That was but the beginning. There is no end to this kind of beginning. You will never

Smith Wigglesworth - JOY Unspeakable and Full of Glory

get an end to the **Holy Ghost** till you are landed in the glory-till you are right in the presence of **God** forever. And even then, we shall ever be conscious of His presence.

God Has Called You Over & Over

Smith Wigglesworth- A **Thankful** heart is a receiving heart; **God** wants to keep you in the place of constant believing with thanksgiving so you will receive.

A dear young Russian came to England. He did not know the language but learned it quickly and was very much used and blessed of **God**. **Wonderful** manifestations of the power of **God** were seen. They pressed upon him to know the secret of his power, but he felt it was so sacred between him and **God**, he should not tell it, but they pressed him so much he finally told them.

"First **God** called me, and His presence was so precious, that I said to **God** at every call I would obey Him, and I yielded, and yielded, and yielded, until I realized that I was simply clothed with another power altogether, and I realized that **God** took me, tongue, thoughts and everything, and I was not myself, but it was **Christ** working through me."

How many of you today have known that **God** has called you over and over, and has put His hand upon you, but you have not yielded in every area of your life? How many of you have had the breathing of His power within you, calling you to prayer, or the meditation of the word and you have to confess that you have failed?

Smith - "You must come to see how **Wonderful** you are in **God** and how helpless you are in yourself."

In another place a woman came to me and said, "I have not been able to smell for twenty years; can you do anything for me?" I said, "You will be able to smell tonight." Could I give anybody that which had been lost for twenty years? Not of myself, but I remembered the Rock on which **God**'s church is built, the Rock **Christ Jesus**, and His promise to give to His own the power to bind and loose.

We can dare to do anything if we know we have the Word of **God** hidden in our hearts, submitted to in every regards. In the name of the **Lord Jesus**, I loosed this woman. She ran all the way home. The table was full of all kinds of good food, but she would not touch a thing. She said, "I am having a feast of just being able to smell again!" **Praise** the **Lord** for the fact that He Himself, **Christ Jesus** backs up his own Word and proves the truth of it in these days of unbelief and apostasy.

Smith - All of me, none of **God**. Less of me, more of **God**. None of me, all of **God**.

At Zurich it was just the same. **God** worked amazing special miracles and wonders. The **Holy Ghost** is different to everyone else. "The anointing ye have

Smith Wigglesworth - JOY Unspeakable and Full of Glory

received abides within you." There was a man with a disease you could not look at. I **praise God** for what **Jesus** does. In just ten minutes he was made whole.

The man sat up in bed and said, "I know I am healed." The doctor came exactly at that time. He was amazed, and said to the man's wife, "Your husband is whole. Whatever has happened? It will not be necessary for me to come anymore." He had been attending his patient three times a day.

In a meeting a young man stood up, a pitiful object, with a face full of sorrow. I said, "What is it, young man?" He said he was unable to work because he could barely walk. He said, "I am so helpless. I have consumption and a weak heart, and my body is full of pain."

I said, "I will pray for you." I said to the people, "As I pray for this young man, I want you to look at his face and see it change."

As I prayed his face changed and there was a **Wonderful** transformation. I said to him, now "Go out and run a mile and come back to the meeting."

He came back and said, "I can now breathe freely." These meetings continuing but I did not seem any longer. After a few days I saw him again in the meeting. I said, "Young man, tell the people what **God** has done for you."

"Oh," he said, "I have been back to work. I bought some papers to sell, and I have made $4.50." **Praise God**, this **Wonderful** stream of salvation never runs dry. You can take a deep drink; it is close to you. It is a river that is running deep and there is plenty for all who are thirsty.

Smith - You are in a great place when you have no-one to turn to but **God**.

A man was brought into one of the meetings in a wheel chair. He could not walk except by the aid of two sticks, and even then, his locomotion was very slow.

I saw him in that helpless condition and told him about **Jesus Christ**. Oh, that **Wonderful** name! Glory to **God**! **"They shall call His name Jesus."** I placed my hands upon his head and said, "In the name of **Jesus** thou art made whole."

This helpless man cried out "It is done, it is done, Glory to **God**, it is done!" And he walked out of the building perfectly healed. The man who brought him in the wheelchair and the children said that **Father** so and so Is walking. **Praise** the **Lord** He is the same yesterday, today and forever.

Smith - "Before a man can bind the enemy, he must know there is nothing binding him."

When I was in Australia a lady came to me who was much troubled about her son who was so lazy and

Smith Wigglesworth - JOY Unspeakable and Full of Glory

refused to work. I prayed over a handkerchief which I had her place on the boy's pillow.

He slept that night on the handkerchief and the next morning he jumped up out of bed and went out and secured a position and went to work. Oh, **praise** the **Lord**, you can't shut **God** out, but if you only believe He will shut the devil out.

Smith - "A man must be in an immoveable condition. The voice of **God** must mean more to him than what he sees, feels or what people say"

One year ago my husband was instantly healed of double rupture of 3 years' standing, dropsy (2 years), a weak heart, and tobacco chewing (47 years), and **praise** the **Lord**, it was all taken away when the power of heaven went straight through him.

Nine weeks ago, today we went to Portland, Oregon, to hear Brother Smith Wigglesworth, and my husband was healed instantly of heavy blood-pressure and varicose veins which had broken in his ankles and for a year had to be dressed twice a day.

No doctor could help him, but, **praise God, Jesus** was the doctor and healed him. Should anyone wish to write me, I shall be **Glad** to hear from them and will answer all letters.-Mrs. Frank Nephews, 202 E. 1st St., Newberg, Ore.

A Report published in Confidence, p. 228-229 December 1914

"I slipped and fell on Broadway, San Diego, in February 1921 I discovered afterwards that I had fractured the base of my spine. I had so severely wrenched the hips and pelvic bones that I was filled with great pain from that moment forward.

As the broken bone was not discovered and set until about two months after the accident, the constant pain and irritation caused a general inflammation of my nervous system, and the long delay in getting the bone set, made it impossible to heal, so that, my condition steadily grew worse, and I was taken to the hospital and the bone was removed about a month after it had been set.

Though the wound healed rapidly, the nervous inflammation remained, and so for many months longer I was in constant pain and unable to get around without assistance. I was taken to the first service held by Mr. Wigglesworth on the 2nd of October 1922.

At the close of the service all those who were sick and in pain and had come for healing were requested to rise if possible. My husband assisted me to my feet, and as those were prayed for by Mister Wigglesworth in the name of **Jesus Christ** I was instantly healed. How I was healed I do not know. I only know the Great Physician touched my body and I was made whole and freed from pain.

Smith Wigglesworth - JOY Unspeakable and Full of Glory

"After I got home, I showed everyone how I could sit down and rise with my hands above my head; when before it had taken both hands to push up my feeble body, and I had to have straps on my bed to pull myself up by. No more use for them now! I lay down and turned over for the first time since the accident without pain.

I shall never cease to **praise God** for the healing of my body through the precious blood of **Jesus** and in His name. I walked to the street car alone the next day and attended the next service and have been "on the go" ever since. To **Jesus** be all the, **praise** and glory." – Mrs. Sanders, 4051 Bay View Court, San Diego, Calif.

Smith - See to it there is never anything comes out of your lips or by your acts that will interfere with the work of the **Lord**

A young woman came into Smith's mission one night and was so impressed with what she heard that at the close she said to Mrs. Wigglesworth: "There is a young woman at Allerton who has been living there for six years and never been outside the door.

Will you go up there?" Mrs. Wigglesworth referred her to her husband, and he said he would go. As he started down the road, which was filled with people traveling to and from, the **Holy Ghost** fell upon him so that he stood in the street and shouted for **JOY**, and the tears rained down his face and saturated his waistcoat.

To his astonishment, nobody in the street seemed to recognize his condition; it seemed as though the **Lord** covered him. He dared not speak to anybody lest the presence of the **Lord** should leave him. The young woman who went with him was full of talk, but he said nothing.

As soon as he entered the house the glory of **God** came more fully upon him and as he lay hands on this poor afflicted woman the glory of **God** filled the house. He was so filled with **God**'s glory he rushed out of the house and the young woman running after him exclaiming, "How did you get this glory? Tell me! Tell me!" He told her to go back into the house and seek the **Lord**.

A week after that he was in an office in Bradford and as soon as he entered the office a man said, "Wigglesworth, sit down. I want to tell you something." He sat down to listen, and the office-man said, "Last Sunday night at the chapel the preacher was during preaching when suddenly the door swung open, and in came a young woman who had been confined to her home for six years.

She stood up and said that as she came out of the house the heavens were covered with the most glorious light and presence of **God**, and she read over the heavens. **'The Lord is coming soon.'"** Mr. Wigglesworth wept and praised **God** but said nothing. He realized that **God** wanted him to know the young lady had been healed but that he was not to talk about it.

Smith Wigglesworth - JOY Unspeakable and Full of Glory

Smith - God wants us so badly that He has made the condition as simple as He possibly could—only believe.

During three weeks thousands daily attended the meetings. Each morning two or three hundred were ministered to for healing. Each evening the platform was surrounded. Again and again, as each throng retired another company came forward seeking salvation. Here many were baptized in the **Holy Ghost**. The testimony meetings were **Wonderful**.

Now I will close with a vision a brother had who attended these meetings. He was lost in intercession for the hundreds of sick waiting to be ministered to for healing. He saw an opening from the platform, where the sick were, right into the glory.

He saw **Wonderful** beings in the form of men resting who, with interest, looked on. Again he looked at the platform and saw a heavenly Being clothed in white, who all the time was more active than any other in helping the sick, and when He touched them the effect was **Wonderful**. Bent forms were made straight, their eyes shone, they began to glorify and **praise** the **Lord**.

A Voice said: "Healings are the smallest of all gifts; it is but a drop in the bucket in view of what **God** has in store for His children. Ye shall do greater works than these."

Last night a dear woman who had been unable to walk for 61 years was brought to be prayed for, and—

glory be to **God**! —she got out of her chair and walked, and her husband pushed her chair along, with her walking behind. **Praise** our covenant-keeping **God**! Truly He is able to do exceedingly abundantly above all that we can ask or think.

There have also been many conversions—at one meeting alone 40 dear ones accepted **Jesus** as their **Lord** and Savior—and we are believing for still greater things. The revival showers are falling and **God** is working. Bless His **Holy** Name!

Just this morning a mother brought her little girl along, who had fallen on a pair of scissors, and cut her mouth so that she could not close it. After the evangelist had laid his hands upon it and prayed, she was able to close her mouth and was quite well. Glory to **God**!

Wigglesworth healing by touch."

An elderly man, who said that he had been deaf for years, cried "**Hallellujah! Hallellujah!**" when asked by Mr. Wigglesworth if he could hear, after hands had been placed on him and he had been prayed over. A woman who, who had stiff legs for over 20 years, and who limped to Olympia on the arm of a relative, ran about the hall in **JOY** after she had been "touched." Another woman, who was said to have been an invalid in a chair for 23 years, declared that her limbs were "beginning to move."

Smith Wigglesworth - JOY Unspeakable and Full of Glory

She was advised by the evangelist to retain her faith in **Jesus Christ** and her cure; would be complete. A young woman with pains of long standing "in her back was able to stoop and touch the ground with her hands, and she laughed heartily as she told the audience that her trouble had gone. A woman, who asserted that she had been unable to walk owing to pain in her feet, ran up and down in front of the audience, crying, "**Praise** the name of the **Lord**." She declared that her pain vanished when the evangelist touched her.

Smith - Hear with the ear of faith! See with the eye of Faith

I was prayed for in Melbourne, and the evil **Spirit** was commanded to come out. I had a polypus growth in my nose. It had been there eighteen years. When I came home from Melbourne the growth broke up and came away, for which I **praise God**.

I had also it pain under my left breast which had troubled me twelve years. I think it was leakage of the heart, as sorrow had caused it in the first place. At times I used to vomit blood. I have deliverance from that also. All **praise** to our wonder-working **Jesus**!   MRS. T. SIMCOCK.

Smith - **God** has something better for you than you have ever had in the past. Come NOW into His fulness, power, life and victory!

A teacher at Bunibank Methodist Sunday school testifies to healing of rheumatoid arthritis. "A doctor examined me in the beginning of December 1911, and told me I would need new joints to walk. He said he would defy anyone to cure me, and although I improved in health I did not walk better.

On April 4th I went to be prayed for and believed **God** would heal me. As hands were placed on my head in the name of **Jesus**, I felt the power of **God** go right through me. After the meeting I walked down three flights of stairs without a stick for the first time for sixteen years, and I have no use for a stick since. I have always tried to impress upon the juniors the power of prayer, but I had not realized I would have to demonstrate it in my own life.

After testifying in the Sunday school, I asked all who were **Christ**ians or who would become one to stand. Every teacher and every scholar stood, and so we sang the Doxology. Men of the world have told me 'It has set them thinking.' There is no evidence now that I had ever rheumatoid arthritis. **Praise God!**"

CHAPTER TWO
(21) QUOTES ON: GOD'S LOVE

"There was never one who came into the world with such loving COMPASSION, and who entered into all the needs of the people as did the **Lord Jesus**. And he declares to us, *'Verily, verily, I say unto you he that believeth on me, the works that I do shall he do also; and greater works than these shall he do, because I go unto my father.'* [Jn 14.12] **God** wants us all to have the audacity of faith that dares to believe for all that is set forth in the word."

"God is gracious and not willing that any should perish."

"**God**'s canopy is over you and will cover you at all times, preserving you from evil."

"Before God could bring me to this place He has broken me a thousand times. I have wept, I have groaned, I have travailed many a night until God broke me. It seems to me that until God has mowed you down you never can have this longsuffering for others. We can never have the gifts of healing and the working of miracles in operation only as we stand in the divine power that God gives us and we stand believing God, and having done all we still stand believing."

"**God** has chosen us to help one another."

"We will be able to succeed only as we do the work in the name of Jesus. Oh, the love that God's Son can put into us if we are only humble enough, weak enough, and helpless enough to know that unless He does it, it will not be done!"

"You must be yielded to the Word of **God**. The Word will work out love in our hearts, and when practical love is in our hearts, there is no room to boast about ourselves. We see ourselves as nothing when we get lost in this divine love."

"If you will but believe, God will meet you and bring into your life the sunshine of His love."

"This Is the Place Where **God** Will Show up! You must come to a place of ashes, a place of helplessness, a place of wholehearted surrender where you do not refer to yourself. You have no justification of your own in regard to anything. You are prepared to be slandered, to be despised by everybody. But because of His personality in you, He reserves you for Himself because you are

Smith Wigglesworth - JOY Unspeakable and Full of Glory

godly, and He sets you on high because you have known His name (Ps. 91:14). He causes you to be the fruit of His loins and to bring forth His glory so that you will no longer rest in yourself. Your confidence will be in **God**. Ah, it is lovely. "The **Lord** is the **Spirit**; and where the **Spirit** of the **Lord** is, there is liberty" (2 Cor. 3:17)."

"Perfect love will never want the preeminence in everything, it will never want to take the place of another, it will always be willing to take the back seat."

"The **God** of all grace, whose very essence is love, delights to liberally give us an inheritance of life, strength and power."

"God is gracious and not willing that any should perish."

"The spiritual life in the believer never has known dissension or break, because where the **Spirit** has perfect liberty, then they all agree and there is no schism in the body."

"The heart is the mainspring."

"Being hardhearted, critical or unforgiving will hinder faith quicker than anything."

"When we get to the place where we take no thought of ourselves, then God takes thought for us."

You cannot bear with others until you know how **God** has borne with you.

"Out of the emptiness, brokenness & yieldedness of our lives, God can bring forth all His glories through us to others."

"See that you never live below the overflowing tide."

"In every weakness, God will be your strength."

I never get out of bed in the morning without having communion with **God** in the **Spirit**.

TEACHING FROM SMITH WIGGLESWORTH

All in Christ will be ready

I also tell you that Paul went so far as to say that some people have very strange ideas of who will be ready for the coming of the KINGDOM. All in **Christ** will be ready, and you have to decide whether you are in **Christ** or not. The Scripture says, in the first verse of Romans 8, "There is therefore now no condemnation to those who are in **Christ Jesus**, who do not walk according to the flesh, but according to the **Spirit**."

If you are there—praise the **Lord**! That is a good position. I ask the **Lord** that He will bring us all into that place. What a wonder it will be. I want you to see that the Master's idea was of a river flowing through everyone who comes to Him. Whatever you think about it, **Jesus** wants your salvation to be like a river, and I am sure that **Jesus** is the ideal for us all.

The lack today is the lack of understanding of that blessed fullness of **Christ**. He came to do nothing less than to embody us with the same manifestation that He had: the manifestation of "doing." Turning for a moment to **Jesus**' attitude in the **Holy Spirit**, I would like you to see a plan there. In Acts 1, we find that **Jesus** "began both to do and teach" (v. 1); the believer should always be

Smith Wigglesworth - JOY Unspeakable and Full of Glory

so full of the **Holy Spirit** that he begins to "do," and then he can "teach." He must be ready for the man in the street. He must be instantly ready, flowing like a river.

He must have three things: ministration, operation, and manifestation, and these three things must always be forthcoming. We ought to be so full of the manifestation of the power of **God** that, in the name of **Jesus**, we can absolutely destroy the power of Satan. We are in the world—not of it (John 17:11, 14). **Jesus** overcame the world (John 16:33), and we are in the world to subdue it unto **God**—as overcomers.

We are nothing in ourselves, but in Christ "we are more than conquerors" (Rom. 8:37) through the blood of **Jesus**—more than a match for satanic powers in every way. Therefore, may the **Lord** let us see that we must be loosed from ourselves. For if you examine yourself, you will be natural, but if you look at **God**, you will be supernatural. always overcoming "him who had the power of death, that is, the devil" (Heb)"

IMPORTANT SCRIPTURES ON GOD'S LOVE

1 Corinthians 13:4-8 - Charity suffereth long, [and] is kind; charity envieth not; charity vaunteth not itself, is not puffed up, (Read More...)

1 Corinthians 16:14 - Let all your things be done with charity.

1 John 4:8 - He that loveth not knoweth not **God**; for **God** is love.

Mark 12:29-31 - And Jesus answered him, The first of all the commandments [is], Hear, O Israel; The Lord our God is one Lord: (Read More...)

Matthew 22:36-40 - Master, which [is] the great commandment in the law? (Read More...)

John 13:34-35 - A new commandment I give unto you, That ye love one another; as I have loved you, that ye also love one another. (Read More...)

Colossians 3:14 - And above all these things [put on] charity, which is the bond of perfectness.

John 15:13 - Greater love hath no man than this, that a man lay down his life for his friends.

John 3:16 - For **God** so loved the world, that he gave his only begotten Son, that whosoever believeth in him should not perish, but have everlasting life.

1 John 4:19 - We love him, because he first loved us.

1 John 4:7 - Beloved, let us love one another: for love is of **God**; and every one that loveth is born of **God**, and knoweth **God**.

1 Peter 4:8 - And above all things have fervent charity among yourselves: for charity shall cover the multitude of sins.

John 14:15 - If ye love me, keep my commandments.

1 John 4:18 - There is no fear in love; but perfect love casteth out fear: because fear hath torment. He that feareth is not made perfect in love.

1 Corinthians 13:1-13 - Though I speak with the tongues of men and of angels, and have not charity, I am become [as] sounding brass, or a tinkling cymbal. (Read More...)

1 Corinthians 13:13 - And now abideth faith, hope, charity, these three; but the greatest of these [is] charity.

Smith Wigglesworth - JOY Unspeakable and Full of Glory

*What a Holy life! What a zeal! What a passion!

O this blessed **Jesus**, the Son of **God**, **Who loved me and gave Himself for me.** This blessed, blessed Son of **God**. I want you to see that we receive sonship because of **His obedience**; because of **His loyalty**; and do not forget what the Scripture says: **"He learned obedience through the things he suffered."**

If you turn to the Scripture you will discover (as incredible as this may sound) that His whole kindred, His mother, brothers, sisters, and the rest of his kindred came and said, **"He is possessed by Beelzebub the devil, and is doing his works."**

See how **Jesus** suffered. They reviled Him and they tried to kill Him by throwing Him over the cliff, but **Jesus** passed through the midst of the whole crowd, and as soon as He was escaped He saw a blind man and healed him as He was going on his Fathers way.

O it is lovely. He is **God**'s example of what can be, and I want to tell you all the attributes and the divine positions and the beatitudes that **Jesus** had. **He was in the world, but not of it.** O it is lovely; it is divinely glorious; and this power of the new creation, this birth unto righteousness by faith in the atonement, can so transform and change you that you can be just like **Jesus Christ**. You can know without a shadow of a doubt that it is Gods power dominating, controlling and filling you and making you like **Jesus**! Understand that though you are still in the body you can be governed by the **Spirit**.

What a **Holy** life! What a zeal! What a passion! 0, to live in all the beauties of all the glory and magnificent of the **Holy Ghost**! **Jesus** was truly the first fruits for us. O, the fascination of the **Christ** of **God** makes me realize there is nothing in this world worth grasping, worth having compared to him. O **Lord**, reveal yourself unto your people. I could never believe it was possible for any man to stand here and preach as I have preached if it was not real to me. I would be ashamed of myself if I did so. But it is not possible.

Beloved, it is the reality of **Christ** that constrains us. There is a constraining power in this blessed **Jesus Christ** of **God** which makes us know that there is something in it that is different from anything in the whole world. It is called in the Scriptures an **"unfeigned love."** It is a tremendously deep word: **"unfeigned love and faith."** Whatever is it?

O beloved, He will tell you what it is. It is a complete denunciation of yourself as the power of **Christ** takes a hold of you, and you feel it would be death to grieve the heart of **God**. You love **God** so deeply that you could stand fire, water or anything in the way of persecution.

He loved you when you were yet sinners, and He seeks your love in return. It is an unfeigned love, a love that can stand ridicule, persecution and slander, because it is a love that is in you by the power of the **Holy Ghost**. He is making you to know that **God** is changing you by His **Spirit** from one state of glory to another state of Glory in the **Holy Ghost**.

I am not at all surprised at His face shining; it is no wonder at the presence of **God** appearing on the Mount, It is no wonder of anything which glorifies the **Christ** of **God**, Who would deny Himself of life to save those of us that were lost in our sins and iniquity.

O what a **Christ**! When we were enemies to Him He died for us! See this very moment that **Jesus** had opportunities which were offered to no other human soul in the world. It was not only the glory of **God** that was offered Him, but the manifestation of a human glory, the offer of which reached Him in the world, for they longed in certain circles to make Him a King.

O, if there was anybody in the world, out of all the countries and nations who was longing to make you a King, you would lose your head and you're commonsense and everything you have to be that king; but our blessed **Christ** of **God** walked away from them, and

Smith Wigglesworth - JOY Unspeakable and Full of Glory

went to secluded prayer. He was the greatest King that ever the world will know.

He is King of Kings and Lord of Lords. 0 yes, and of **His KINGDOM there shall be no end, and He shall see His seed; He shall prolong His days, and the pleasure of the Lord shall prosper in His hands.**

I wonder if there is any of the seed of the **Lord Jesus** in this place. 0 you that believe you are the seed of the Son of **God** through faith in Gods promise. The seed of the Son of **God**, by faith in **Christ**. The seed of the Son of **God** because His seed is in you, which is the Word of **God**, and you are saved by His power. All the seed in this place, let us see your hands. He shall see His seed; He shall prolong His days, and the pleasure of the **Lord** shall prosper in His hands. O **Hallellujah**!

THE FRUIT OF THE SPIRIT!

There is a fruit of the **Spirit** that must accompany the gift of healing and that is longsuffering. The man who is going through with **God** to be used in healing must be a man of longsuffering. He must be always ready with a word of comfort. If the sick one is in distress and helpless and does not see everything eye to eye with you, you must bear with him. Our **Lord Jesus Christ** was filled with COMPASSION and lived and moved in a place of longsuffering, and we will have to get into this place if we are to help needy ones.

There are some times when you pray for the sick and you are apparently rough. But you are not dealing with a person, you are dealing with the Satanic forces that are binding the person. Your heart is full of love and COMPASSION to all, but you are moved to a **Holy** anger as you see the place the devil has taken in the body of the sick one, and you deal with his position with a real forcefulness. One day a pet dog followed a lady out of her house and ran all round her feet.

She said to the dog, "My dear, I cannot have you with me today." The dog wagged its tail and made a big fuss. She said, "Go home, my dear." But the dog did not go. At last she shouted roughly, "Go home," and off it went. Some people deal with the devil like that, The devil can stand all the comfort you like to give him. Cast him out!

You are dealing not with the person, you are dealing with the devil. Demon power must be dislodged in the name of the **Lord**. You are always right when you dare to deal with sickness as with the devil. Much sickness is caused by some misconduct, there is something wrong, there is some neglect somewhere, and Satan has had a chance to get in. It is necessary to repent and confess where you have given place to the devil, and then he can be dealt with.

"Father, forgive them."

They stoned Stephen, who called upon **God** and said, **"Lord Jesus, receive my Spirit."** And he kneeled down, and cried with a loud voice, **"Lord, lay not this sin to their charge."** And when he had said this he fell asleep. Stephen was not only filled with faith but he was also filled with love as he prayed just as his Master prayed, **"Father, forgive them."**

It is **God**'s thought to make us a new creation, with all the old things passed away and all things within us truly of **God**, to bring in a new divine order, a perfect love and an unlimited faith. Will you have it? Redemption is free. Arise in the activity, the operation, and the power of faith and **God** will heal you as you arise.

Only believe and receive in faith all that **God** has promised you. **Stephen, full of faith and of the Holy Ghost, did great signs and**

Smith Wigglesworth - JOY Unspeakable and Full of Glory

wonders. May **God** bless us with this revelation of his will and fill us full of His **Holy Spirit**. And through the power of the **Holy Ghost** reveal to us **Christ** in us.

The **Holy Ghost** of **God** will always reveal the **Lord Jesus Christ**. Serve Him, love Him, be filled with Him. It is lovely to hear Him as He makes Himself known to us. **He is the same yesterday, today and forever.** He is willing to fill us with the **Holy Ghost** and faith just as He filled Stephen.

The Power of the Name

One day I went up into the mountain to pray. I had a **Wonderful** day. It was one of the high mountains of Wales. I heard of one man going up this mountain to pray, and the **Spirit** of the **Lord** met him so wonderfully that his face shone like that of an angel when he came back. Everyone in the village was talking about it. As I went up to this mountain and spent the day in the presence of the **Lord**, His **Wonderful** power seemed to envelop, saturate, overwhelm and fill me.

Two years before this time there had come to our house two lads from Wales. They were just ordinary lads, but they became very zealous for **God**. They came to our mission and saw some of the works of **God**. They said to me, "We would not be surprised if the **Lord** brings you down to Wales to raise up our Lazarus." They explained that the leader of their assembly was a man who had spent his days working in a tin mine and his nights preaching, and the result was that he had collapsed, gone into consumption, and for four years he had been a helpless invalid, having to be fed with a spoon.

While I was up on that mountain top I was reminded of the transfiguration scene, and I felt that the **Lord**'s only purpose in taking us into the glory was to fit us for greater usefulness in the valley. Now as I was on this mountain top that day, the **Lord** said to me, "I want you to go and raise Lazarus." I told the brother who accompanied me what the **Lord** told me, and when we got down to the valley, I wrote a postcard: "When I was up on the mountain praying today, **God** told me that I was to go and raise Lazarus." I addressed the postcard to the man in the place whose name had been given to me by the two lads.

When we arrived at the place we went to the man to whom I had addressed the card to. He looked at me and said, "Did you send this?" I said, "Yes." He said, "Do you think we believe in this? Here, take it." And he threw it at me.

The man called a servant and said, "Take this man and show him Lazarus." Then he said to me, "The moment you see him you will be ready to go home. Nothing will keep you here then." Everything he said was true from the natural viewpoint. The man was completely helpless. He was nothing but a mass of bones with skin stretched over them. There was no life to be seen at all. Everything in him spoke of decay and death.

I said to him, "Will you shout? You remember that at Jericho the people shouted while the walls were still up. **God** has the same type of victory for you if you will only believe." But I could not get him to believe not even an ounce. There was not an atom of faith in his heart. He had decided in his mind that there was no hope.

It is a blessed thing to learn that **God**'s word can never fail. Never hearken to human plans or ideals. **God** can work mightily when you persist in believing Him in spite of discouragements from the human standpoint. When I got back to the man to whom I had sent the post-card, he asked, "Are you ready to go now?"

I told him I am not moved by what I see. I am moved only by what I believe. I know this for a fact that no man who was walking by faith looks at the circumstances if he believes. No man considers how he feels if he believes. The man who believes **God** has victory in every situation.

Smith Wigglesworth - JOY Unspeakable and Full of Glory

Every man who comes into the fullness of the **Spirit** can laugh at all things and believe **God**. There is something in the full gospel work that is different from anything else in the world. Somehow, in Pentecost, you know that **God** is a reality. Wherever the **Holy Ghost** has His way, the gifts of the **Spirit** will be in manifestation; and where these gifts are never in manifestation, I question whether He is present. **Holy Ghost** people are spoiled for anything else than **Holy Ghost** meetings. We want none of the entertainments that the churches are offering. When **God** comes in He entertains us Himself. Entertained by the King of kings and **Lord** of lords! O, it is **Wonderful**.

There were spiritually difficult conditions in that Welsh village, and it seemed impossible to get the people to believe. "Ready to go home?" I was asked. But a man and a woman there asked us to come and stay with them. I said, "I want to know how many of you people can pray." No one wanted to pray. I asked if I could get seven people to pray with me for the poor man's deliverance.

I said to the two people who were going to entertain us, "I will count on you two, and there is my friend and myself, and we need three others." I told the people that I trusted that some of them would awaken to their responsibility and come in the morning and join us in prayer for the raising of Lazarus. It will never do to give way to human opinions. If **God** says a thing, you are to believe it. Never even asked people what they think, because all the abundance of their heart they will utter their unbelief.

I told the people that I would not eat anything that night. When I went to bed it seemed as if the devil tried to place on me everything that he had placed on that poor man in the bed. When I awoke I had a cough and all the weakness of a tubercular patient. I rolled out of bed on to the floor and cried out to **God** to deliver me from the power of the devil.

I shouted loud enough to wake everybody in the house, but nobody was disturbed. **God** gave me **Wonderful** victory, and I got back into bed again as free as ever I was in my life. At 5 o'clock the **Lord** awakened me and said to me, "Don't break bread until you break it round my table." At 6 o'clock He gave me these words, "And I will raise him up." I put my elbow into the fellow who was sleeping with me. He said, "Ugh!" I put my elbow into him again and said, "Do you hear? The **Lord** says that He will raise Lazarus up."

At 8 o'clock they said to me, "Have a little refreshment." But I have found prayer and fasting the greatest **JOY**, and you will always find it so when you are led by **God**. When we went to the house where Lazarus lived there were eight of us altogether. No one can prove to me that **God** does not always answer prayer. He always does more than we ask or think. He always gives exceedingly abundant above all we ask or think.

I shall never forget how the power of **God** fell on us as we went into that sick man's room. O, it was lovely! As we circled round the bed I got one brother to hold one of the sick man's hands and I held the other; and we each held the hand of the person next to us. I said, "We are not going to pray, we are just going to use the name of **Jesus**." We all knelt down and whispered that one word, "**Jesus! Jesus! Jesus!**"

The power of **God** fell and then it lifted. Five times the power of **God** fell and then it remained. But the person who was in the bed was unmoved. Two years previous someone had come along and had tried to raise him up, and the devil had used his lack of success as a means of discouraging him. I said, "I don't care what the devil says; if **God** says he will raise you up it must be so. Forget everything else except what **God** says about **Jesus**."

The sixth time the power fell and the sick man's lips began moving and the tears began to fall. I said to him, "The power of **God** is here; it is yours to accept it." He said, "I have been bitter in my heart, and I know I have grieved the **Spirit** of **God**. Here I am helpless. I cannot lift my hands, nor even lift a spoon to my mouth." I said, "Repent, and **God** will hear you." He repented and cried out, "O **God**, let this be to Thy glory." As he said this the virtue of the **Lord** went right through him.

Smith Wigglesworth - JOY Unspeakable and Full of Glory

I have asked the **Lord** to never let me tell this story except as it was, for I realize that **God** cannot bless exaggerations. As we again said, "**Jesus! Jesus! Jesus!**" the bed shook, and the man shook. I said to the people that were with me, "You can all go down stairs right away. This is all **God**. I'm not going to assist him." I sat and watched that man get up and dress himself. We sang the doxology as he walked down the steps. I said to him, "Now tell what has happened."

It was soon noised abroad that Lazarus had been raised up from the bed of death and the people came from Llanelly and all the district around to see him and hear his testimony. **God** brought salvation to many. This man preached right out in the open air what **God** had done, and as a result many were convicted and converted. All this came through the name of **Jesus**, through faith in His name, yea, the faith that is by Him gave this sick man perfect soundness in the presence of them all.

PASSION FOR CHRIST

BY DR MICHAEL H YEAGER

I would say that these men are dedicated and passionate for **Jesus Christ**, but listen, there are many different levels of **Passion**. So let me encourage you with a strong word. If you want to go to another dimension, you have got to have a greater commitment. You must have deeper **Passion**.

I'm convinced when Paul said: I have not yet apprehended all that **God** has for me. He was saying I am not yet near as passionate as what I can be! Now, I am talking about being passionate four **God**. A lot of **Christ**ians are passionate for certain crusades. I understand these things, but our **Passion** is for **God**. Our **Passion** is for **Jesus Christ**. How much are we to love **God**? With all our hearts, souls, mind, emotions and our whole being. That means it affects every part of our existence, mentally, physically, emotionally, financially, and socially.

Now, what does it look like when you get to that place? It looks just like **Jesus Christ** because **Jesus** loved his **Father** with everything. All His heart, all of his soul, all of his mind, all of his strength and all of his being. Therefore, the Bible says you are carnal if you are comparing yourself one to another. I strive never to compare myself to anybody else but to **Jesus Christ**.

Am I as passionate as **Jesus**? Am I operating the same place? Will I ever apprehend all the **Passion** that **Jesus** had in this life? No, I'll never, but I am sure going to try! I am not talking about trying to get an experience or a manifestation or a visitation. I will get them. I will have them, but it can only be to the degree of my **Passion** for **Jesus** and for the truth.

Jesus is the truth, the way, the light. It is not **God** that determines whether you are going to be going deeper in the things of **Christ**. **God**'s not the one who's determining whether you're going to go deeper.

I think Smith Wigglesworth is a perfect example of this. Smith up until he was 48 years old was simply a plumber. He gave his heart to **Christ** when he was eight years old. He did have a **Passion** for souls as a young boy. He was a soul winner, but he didn't get filled with the **Holy Ghost** until he was 48 years old. In his sermons

Smith Wigglesworth - JOY Unspeakable and Full of Glory

he revealed that he had grown cold towards **God**. His wife Polly was the minister of the mission where they attended. He reveals in his sermons that he had a terrible temper that would just explode. In those days they did not have anger management.

Smith had a real bad temper but when he was filled with the **Holy Ghost** and he became passionate for **God**, the **Lord** delivered him from his terrible anger. Smith went to the new level in the fruit of the **Spirit**. By the time he died, at 87 he went to a place that 99.9% of believers will never go. Smith saw amputated limbs growing out. He went to schools of the blind, praying for all the blind people. They were all healed. He went to places for the mentally insane, and everyone was healed

So here is the **Wonderful** news. If Smith Wigglesworth was not very spiritual up till, he was 48 years old, but he became mightily used of **God** up till he was 87 there is hope for you and me. If his **Passion** could grow starting at 48 years old, there's hope for all of us.

This word is full of Life
Smith Wigglesworth

Stimulation—brought by faith into a place of grace where all may see us made anew. If you believe, you can be sons of **God**—in likeness, character, **Spirit**, longings, acts, until all will know you are a son of **God**. The **Spirit** of God can change our nature. **God** is Creator. His Word is creative, and as you believe, a creative power is changing your whole nature. You can reach this altitude only by faith. No man can keep himself. The **God** of almightiness spreads His covering over you, saying, "I am able to do all things; and all things are possible to him that believeth."

The old nature is so difficult to manage. You have been ashamed of it many a time, but the **Lord** Himself will come. He says, "Come unto Me, and I will give you rest, peace, strength. I will change you, I will operate upon you by My power making you a new creation, if you will believe."

Take your burden to the **Lord** and leave it there. **"Learn of Me for I am meek and lowly in heart, and ye shall find rest unto your souls."** The world has no rest, it is full of trouble; but in Him is peace which passeth understanding, with an inward flow of divine power changing your nature until you can live, move and act in the power of **God**.

"Therefore the world knoweth us not because it knew Him not." What does it mean? I have lived in one house over fifty years. I have preached from my own doorstep, and all around know me. They know. me when they need someone to pray, when there is trouble, when they need help. But at Christmas time, when they call their friends, would they call me? No! Why? They would say, "He is sure to want a prayer meeting, but we want to finish up with a dance."

Wherever **Jesus** came sin was revealed and men don't like sin revealed. Sin, separates from **God** for ever. You are in a good place when you weep before **God**, repenting over the least thing. If you have spoken unkindly, you realize it was not like the **Lord**. Your keen conscience has taken you to prayer. It is a **Wonderful** thing to have a keen conscience. It is when we are close to **God** that our hearts are revealed. **God** intends us to live in purity—seeing Him all the time.

"Beloved, now are we the sons of God, and it doth not yet appear what we shall be; but we know that when He shall appear we shall be like Him for we shall see Him as He is; and everyone that hath this hope purifieth himself even as He is pure."

It is the hope of the Church, the Bridegroom coming for the bride. He has suffered for us, been buried for us, risen for us, is jealous for us. How we should love Him! He is coming again and He wants us to be ready.

Smith Wigglesworth - JOY Unspeakable and Full of Glory

"You must be yielded to the Word of God. The Word will work out love in our hearts, and when practical love is in our hearts, there is no room to boast about ourselves. We see ourselves as nothing when we get lost in this divine love."

There are many dry places. Indeed, nearly every town I go to is said to be the driest of places—"the hardest town in the KINGDOM," they will say. What is that to do with you? **The Lord's hand is not shortened that it cannot save. [Is 59.1]** It is in man's extremity that **God** finds his greatest opportunity. It is for his word to awaken his beloved church; and so **God** wants us with great hope! **"All things are possible to them that believe." Mk 9.23**

Treasury of the Most High

I believe that if there is anything that **God** is dissatisfied with, it is our settling down into a stationary condition. We stop on the threshold, when **God** in His great plan is inviting us into His treasury. Oh, this treasury of the Most High, the unsearchable riches of **Christ**, this divine position which **God** wants to move us into, so that we are altogether a new creation, the old self-life having passed away, where we are dead unto sin but alive unto **God** through **Jesus Christ** our **Lord**!

There is one thing that hinders, and that is the carnal mind, which is enmity against **God**. But there is a glorious victory over carnality through the cross of **Christ**. My Bible tells me that my old man with all his carnality was crucified with **Christ**. At the cross of **Christ** there is victory complete and full over all the old self-life. **God** wants us to know the resurrection power of the **Lord**, and to bring us into a place of rest, of faith, of **JOY** and peace and blessing and of fullness of life; the very same **Spirit** which raised up **Christ** from the dead quickening our mortal bodies so that we are full and overflowing with the life of **Christ** Himself.

May the **Lord** give us a new vision of Himself, and such a fullness of His divine life that we will shake off all that remains of the old life. Let us pray that He may bring us fully into all the newness of life. May He reveal to us the greatness of His will concerning us for there is no one who loves us as **Jesus**, there is no love like His, no COMPASSION like His. He is filled with love and never fails to take those who fully obey Him into the promised land.

Beloved, in **God**'s Word there is always more to follow, always more than we can know, and if we will allow the **Spirit** of **God** to take us into all that is in the mind of **God** for us, what **Wonderful** things will happen. Do not merely take a part of the Bible, take it all. When we get such a thirst upon us that nothing can satisfy us but **God**, we have a royal time.

If you are a child of **God** do not be satisfied with anything less than reality all the time. **God** has His hidden treasures for those who seek Him. Are you dry? There is no dry place in **God**, but all the good things come out of hard times. The harder the place you are in, the more blessedness can come out of it, as you yield to His plan. **God** is so abundant, so full of love and mercy; there is no lack to them that trust in Him.

What works in us through being one with him, rooted and grounded? Perfect love, and perfect love has justice wrapped up in it, and the day is coming when the saints will say "Amen" to the judgments of God.

.

CHAPTER THREE

Let me tell you something, if you get a **Passion** for **Jesus** and the truth, miracles will come. Smith Wigglesworth said until you get a **Passion** for **Christ**, you will never see a lot of miracles. People are trying to work miracles, without a **Passion** for **Jesus**. Get **Passion** for **Christ** and the miracles will flow like a mighty river. **Jesus** said to the church in revelation, chapter three: Doc Yeager

Revelation 3:15 I know thy works, that thou art neither cold nor hot: I would thou wert cold or hot. 16 So then because thou art lukewarm, and neither cold nor hot, I will spue thee out of my mouth. 17 Because thou sayest, I am rich, and increased with goods, and have need of nothing; and knowest not that thou art wretched, and miserable, and poor, and blind, and naked:

SMITH WIGGLESWORTH

Smith - It is my business to make people either Glad or mad. I have a message from heaven that will not leave people as I find them.

"I don't ever ask Smith Wigglesworth how he feels!" I jump out of bed! I dance before the Lord for at least 10 to 12 minutes – high speed dancing. I jump up and down and run around my room telling God how great he is, how Wonderful He is, how Glad I am to be associated with Him and to be His child."

"If you leave people as you found them, God is not speaking by you. If you are not making people mad or Glad, there is something amiss with your ministry. If there is not a war taking place, it means you're doing a bad."

I love to do the will of God; there is no irksomeness to it; it is no trial to pray; no trouble to read the Word of God; it is not a hard thing to go to the place of worship. With the psalmist you say, "I was Glad when they said unto me, Let us go into the house of the Lord."

Smith- "Some people like to read their Bibles in the Hebrew; some like to read it in the Greek; I like to always ready it in the Holy Spirit."

Smith Wigglesworth - JOY Unspeakable and Full of Glory

One morning our children were all gathered around the breakfast table and my wife said, "Harold and Ernest are very sick this morning. Before we have breakfast we will go pray for them." Immediately the power of **God** fell upon my wife and me, and as we laid our hands on our children they were both instantly healed. As we saw the miraculous healing wrought before our eyes, we were both filled with intense **JOY**. The **Lord** was always so good in proving Himself our family Physician.

JOY CAME AT HIS HEALING

Smith - "If you want to increase in the life of God, then you must settle it in your heart that you will not at any time resist the Holy Spirit. The Holy Ghost and fire - the fire burning up everything that would hurt and destroy your walk with God."

I will never forget the face of a man that came to me one time. His clothes hung from him, his whole frame was shrivelled, and his eyes were glaring and glassy, his jawbones stuck out, his whole being was a manifestation of death. He said to me, "Can you help me?" Could I help him?

I told him if we believe the **Word of God** can we help anybody, but we must be sure we are basing our faith on the Word of **God**. If we are on the Word of **God** then what **God** has promised will happen. I looked at him and I told him that I had never seen anybody that was still alive that looked like him. I said, "What is wrong with you? He answered with a small whisper of a voice, "I had a cancer in my chest. I was operated on and in removing this cancer they also removed my swallower; so now I can breathe but I cannot swallow."

He pulled out a tube about nine inches long with a cup at the top and an opening at the bottom to go into a hole. He showed me that he pressed one part of that into his stomach and poured liquid into the top; it was like he was a walking dead man. I said to him:"

... whosoever ... shall not doubt in his heart, but shall believe that those things which he saith shall come to pass; he shall have saith" (Mark 11:23).

Based upon this reality I said to him "You shall have a good supper tonight." But, he said "I cannot swallow." I said, "You shall
have a good supper tonight." But he repeated "I cannot swallow." ..... I said, "You shall have a good supper; now go and eat."

When he got home he told his wife that the preacher said he could eat a good supper that night. He said, "If you will get something ready I'll see if I can swallow." His wife prepaired a good supper and he took a mouthful. When he had tried to eat before the food would not go down. But the Word of **God** said "whatsoever," and this mouthful went down, and more and more went down until he was completely filled up! Then what happened? He went to bed with the **JOY** of the knowledge that he could again swallow, and he awoke the next morning with the same **JOY**! He looked for the hole in his stomach, but **God** had shut that hole in his stomach up.

Smith - "Never listen to human plans. God can work mightily when you persist in believing Him in spite of discouragement from the human standpoint. ... I am moved by what I believe. I know this: no man looks at the circumstances if he believes."

I know of a situation where six people went into the house of a sick man to pray for him. He was an Episcopalian priest, and he laid in his bed utterly helpless, without even strength to help himself. He had read a little tract about Divine healing and had heard about people praying for the sick, and sent for some of my friends, who, he thought, could pray the prayer of faith. He was anointed according to *James 5:14*, but, he had no immediate manifestation of healing, he wept bitterly. The six people walked out of the room, somewhat discouraged to see the man lying there in an unchanged condition.

When they were outside, one of the six said, "There is one thing we should have done. I wish you would all go back with me and let's try it." They all went back and got together in a group. This brother said, "Let us whisper the name of **Jesus**." At first when they whispered this **Wonderful** worthy name nothing seemed to happen. But as they continued to whisper, **"Jesus!**

Jesus! Jesus! In Faith , sincerity and Love" the power of **God** began to fall.

As they saw that **God** was beginning to work, their faith and **JOY** increased; and they whispered the name of **Jesus Christ** louder and louder. As they did so the man suddenly arose from his bed and dressed himself. The secret was simply this, those six people had got their eyes off the sick man, and put their eyes upon the **Lord Jesus** Himself, their faith grasped the power and authority that there is in the name that's above every name of **Jesus Christ** of Nazareth.

Smith - "The Bible is the Word of God: supernatural in origin, eternal in duration, inexpressible in valor, infinite in scope, regenerative in power, infallible in authority, universal in interest, personal in application, inspired in totality. Read it through, write it down, pray it in, work it out, and then pass it on. Truly it is the Word of God. It brings into man the personality of God; it changes the man until he becomes the epistle of God. It transforms his mind, changes his character, takes him on from grace to grace, and gives him an inheritance in the Spirit. God comes in, dwells in, walks in, talks through, and sups with him."

Spiritual Power

A woman came to me in Cardiff, Wales, who was filled with an ulceration. She had fallen in the streets twice through this trouble. She came to the meeting and it seemed as if the evil power within her was trying to kill her right there, for she fell, and the power of the devil was extremely brutal. She was helpless, and it seemed as if she had died right there on the spot. I cried,

"O **God**, help this woman." Then I rebuked the evil power in the name of **Jesus**, and instantly right then and there the **Lord** healed her. She rose up and was so filled with excitement and **JOY** that we could not keep her quiet. She felt the power of **God** in her body and wanted to testify all the time.

After three days she went to another place and began to testify about the **Lord**'s power to heal the sick and the demonically oppressed. She came to me and said, "I want to tell everyone about the **Lord**'s healing power. Have you no tracts on this subject?" I handed her my Bible and said, "Matthew, Mark, Luke, John--they are the best tracts on healing.

They are full of incidents about the power of **Jesus**. They will never fail to accomplish the work of **God** if people will believe

JOY AT THE BAPTISM OF THE HOLY GHOST

Smith - Never mind what it costs - it is worth everything to have His smile and His presence

It was about thirty-one years ago that a man came to me and said, "Wigglesworth, do you know what is happening in Sunderland? People are being baptized in the **Holy Ghost** exactly the same way as the disciples were on the Day of Pentecost." I said, "I would like to go." I immediately took a train and went to Sunderland. I went to the meetings and said, "I want to hear these tongues." I was told, "When you receive the Baptism in the **Holy Ghost**, you will speak in tongues." I said, "I have the Baptism in the **Holy Ghost**."

One man said, "Brother, when I received the Baptism I spoke in tongues." I said, "Let's hear you." But could not speak in tongues, he could only speak as the **Spirit** gave him utterance and so my curiosity was not satisfied.

I saw these people were very earnest and I became quite hungry. I was anxious to see this new manifestation of the **Spirit** and I would be questioning all the time and spoiling a lot of the meetings. One man said to me, "I am a missionary and I have come here to seek the Baptism in the **Holy Ghost**.

I am waiting on the **Lord**, but you have come in and are spoiling everything with your questions." I began to argue with him and our love became so hot that when we walked home he walked on one side of the road and I on the other.

That night there was to be a waiting meeting and I purposed to go. I changed my clothes and left my key in the clothes I had taken off. As we came from the meeting in the middle of the night I found I did not have my key upon me and this missionary brother said, "You will have to come and sleep with me." But do you think we went to bed that night? Oh, no, we spent the night in prayer.

Smith Wigglesworth - JOY Unspeakable and Full of Glory

We received a precious shower from above. The breakfast bell rang, but I was not hungry. For four days I wanted nothing but **God**. If you only knew the unspeakably **Wonderful** blessings of being filled with the Third Person of the Trinity, you would set aside everything else to tarry for this infilling.

I was about to leave Sunderland. This revival was taking place in the vestry of an Episcopal Church. I went to the parsonage that day to say goodbye and I said to Sister Boddy, the vicar's wife, "I am going away, but I have not received the tongues yet." She said, "It isn't tongues you need, but the Baptism." I said, "I have the Baptism, Sister, but I would like to have you lay hands on me before I leave."

She laid her hands on me and then had to go out of the room. The fire fell. It was a **Wonderful** time as I was there with **God** alone. It seemed as though **God** bathed me in power. I was given a **Wonderful** vision. I was conscious of the cleansing of the precious blood and cried out, "Clean! Clean! Clean!"

I was filled with the **JOY** of the consciousness of the cleansing. I saw the **Lord Jesus Christ**. I saw the empty cross and I saw Him exalted at the right hand of **God** the Father. As I was extolling, magnifying, and praising Him I was speaking in tongues as the **Spirit** of **God** gave me utterance. I knew now that I had received the real Baptism in the **Holy Ghost**.

I sent a telegram home and when I got there one of our boys said, "Father, I hear you have been speaking in tongues. Let's hear you." I could not speak in tongues. I had been moved to speak in tongues as the **Spirit** of **God** gave utterance at the moment I received the Baptism, but I did not receive the gift of tongues and could not speak a word. I never spoke again in tongues until nine months later when I was praying for someone, and it was then that **God** gave me the permanent gift of speaking in tongues.

When I got home my wife said to me, "So you think you have received the Baptism of the **Holy Ghost**. Why, I am as much baptized in the **Holy Ghost** as you are." We had sat on the platform together for twenty years but that night she said, "Tonight you will be preaching to the congregation."

I said, "All right." As I went up to the platform that night the **Lord** gave me the first few verses of the sixty-first chapter of Isaiah, "The **Spirit** of the **Lord God** is upon me; because the **Lord** hath anointed me to preach good tidings unto the meek: He hath sent me to bind up the broken-hearted, to proclaim liberty to the captives, and the opening of the prison to them that are bound."

My wife went back to one of the furthermost seats in the hall and she said to herself, "I will watch what happens." I preached that night on the subject the **Lord** had given me and I told what the **Lord** had done for me. I told the people that I was going to have **God** in my life and I would gladly suffer a thousand deaths rather than forfeit this **Wonderful** infilling that had come to me.

My wife was very restless. She was moved in a new way and said, "That is not my Smith that is preaching. **Lord**, you have done something for him." As soon as I

Smith Wigglesworth - JOY Unspeakable and Full of Glory

had finished, the secretary of the mission got up and said, "Brethren, I want what the leader of our mission has got." He tried to sit down but missed his seat and fell on the floor.

There were soon fourteen of them on the floor, my own wife included. We did not know what to do, but the **Holy Ghost** got hold of the situation and the fire fell. A revival started and the crowds came. It was only the beginning of the flood-tide of blessing. We had touched the reservoir of the **Lord**'s life and power. Since that time the **Lord** has taken me to many different lands and I have witnessed many blessed outpourings of **God**'s **Holy Spirit**.

CHAPTER FOUR

(14) QUOTES ON: DIVINE NATURE

SMITH WIGGLESWORTH

"Jesus was only laying a foundation, which is the new birth unto righteousness. It is the drink at the well; it is receiving Him, and by receiving Him, you may have power to become children of God. For as many as receive Him become the children of God (John 1:12)."

"**God** wants to purify our minds until we can bear all things, believe all things, hope all things and endure all things. **God** dwells in you, but you cannot have this divine power until you live and walk in the **Holy Ghost**, until the power of the new life is greater than the old life."

Smith Wigglesworth - JOY Unspeakable and Full of Glory

"There is something a thousand times better than feelings, and it is the powerful Word of God. There is a divine revelation within you that came when you were born from above, and this is real faith. To be born into the new KINGDOM is to be born into a new faith."

"One half of the trouble in the assemblies is the people's murmuring over the conditions they are in. The Bible teaches us not to murmur. If you reach that standard, you will never murmur anymore. You will be above murmuring.

You will be in the place where **God** is absolutely the exchanger of thought, the exchanger of actions, and the exchanger of your inward purity. He will be purifying you all the time and lifting you higher, and you will know you are not of this world (John 15:19)."

"Wigglesworth, like Charles Finney, believed that the presence of a man filled with God could bring conviction to sinners without even a word being spoken. As he sat opposite a man in a railway carriage, the man suddenly jumped up, exclaimed, 'You convict me of sin!' and went out into another carriage."

"Before God could bring me to this place He has broken me a thousand times. I have wept, I have groaned, I have travailed many a night until God broke me. It seems to me that until God has mowed you down you never can have this longsuffering for

others.

We can never have the gifts of healing and the working of miracles in operation only as we stand in the divine power that God gives us and we stand believing God, and having done all we still stand believing."

This Is the Place Where **God** Will Show up! You must come to a place of ashes, a place of helplessness, a place of wholehearted surrender where you do not refer to yourself. You have no justification of your own in regard to anything. You are prepared to be slandered, to be despised by everybody.

But because of His personality in you, He reserves you for Himself because you are godly, and He sets you on high because you have known His name (Ps. 91:14). He causes you to be the fruit of His loins and to bring forth His glory so that you will no longer rest in yourself. Your confidence will be in **God**. Ah, it is lovely. "The **Lord** is the **Spirit**; and where the **Spirit** of the **Lord** is, there is liberty" (2 Cor. 3:17).

"Beloved, if you read the Scriptures you will never find anything about the easy time. All the glories come out of hard times. And if you are really reconstructed it will be in a hard time, it won't be in a singing meeting, but at a time when you think all things are dried up, when you think there is no hope for you.

Smith Wigglesworth - JOY Unspeakable and Full of Glory

And you have passed everything, then that is the time that God makes the man, when tried by fire, that God purges you, takes the dross away, and brings forth the pure gold. Only melted gold is minted. Only moistened clay receives the mold. Only softened wax receives the seal. Only broken, contrite hearts receive the mark as the Potter turns us on His wheel, shaped and burnt to take and keep the heavenly mold, the stamp of God's pure gold."

"There is a fruit of the **Spirit** that must accompany the gift of healing and that is longsuffering."

"The man who is going through with God to be used in healing must be a man of longsuffering."

"You must come to see how **Wonderful** you are in **God** and how helpless you are in yourself."

"Once on a train, the Spirit was so heavily upon me that my face shone. Within 3 minutes, everyone on the train was crying to God."

"The **Lord** will allow you to be very drunk in His presence, but sober among people."

"Forgive, and the Lord will forgive you."

Abiding Spirit

An address given in Adelaide by Evang. S. Wigglesworth
Luke 9:27 But I tell you of a truth, there be some standing here, which shall not taste of death, till they see the KINGDOM of God.

If you had any idea how **God** seems to fascinate me with His Word. I read and read and read, and yet there is always something so new, remarkable and blessed that I find it is true what the Scriptures says. As I get deeper into the knowledge of the Bridegroom, I hear the voice of **Jesus** saying,

"The Bride rejoices to hear the Bridegroom's voice." The Word is **"His Voice,"** and, as we get nearer to **Jesus**, we understand the principles of His mission; that He came to take out for Himself a people that they might be called **"His Bride." He came to find "a Body."** **God**'s message to us to-night is that He is going to take out of His body a Bride unto Himself, and so I believe that while we talk about salvation there are deeper truths that **God** wants to show us.

It is not only to be saved, my brother, but that there is an eternal destiny awaiting us of wonderment that **God** has for us in the glory. I pray that we may be so interested in this evening's service that we may see, that **God** in His mercy has given to us this blessed revelation of how He lived, loved and had the power to say to those disciples, **"Some of you shall not see death till ye have seen the KINGDOM of God coming in power."** Oh our blessed **Christ**!—Who could pray till the completeness of His countenance was transformed and

Smith Wigglesworth - JOY Unspeakable and Full of Glory

became glorious; till His raiment and all about Him was wonderfully changed" and become glistening! Praise the **Lord** for a Savior, Who so lived in heart and fellowship with **God** that He had power to say these things.

Also He said, **"I have power to lay down My life, and I have power to take it again."** It is truly said that by wicked hands He was taken and crucified; but He had to be willing, for He had all power, and could have called on legions of angels to help Him and deliver Him from death; but O that blessed **Christ**, our **Wonderful** savior, had purposed in his heart to save us, and to bring us into fellowship and oneness with **God** the Father in order to give to us the divine principles of life, and life more abundantly.

Our blessed Savior of **God** never looked back; never withheld. He went right through to death in order that He might impart into us this blessed reconciliation between **God** and man. So it was the man, **Christ Jesus**, Who is the atonement for the whole world; the **Christ** of **God**; the Son of **God**; who is the sinner's friend. He was wounded for our transgressions. This **Jesus** meant all He said while He lived.

He lived to manifest and bring forth the glory of **God** to earth. This blessed **Christ** gave His disciples the glory which He had with the Father before the world was. He said, **"I have given them the glory which Thou gavest Me."** O, He is lovely, and I believe that **God** wants us to know that while **God** is giving grace and glory**; no good thing will He withhold from them that walk uprightly;** health and peace; **JOY** in the **Holy Ghost**; a life in 'Christ Jesus.

O, how **Wonderful** He is! How lovely! Shall we go back into Egypt? **Never!** Shall we look back? **Never!** What shall we do? "O, you will never find me in Egypt's sand, for I have pitched my tent far up in Beulah land." O brother, O sister, **God** wants you to know that He has a redemption for you through the Blood of **Jesus Christ**, which is heaven on earth; which is **JOY** and peace in the **Holy Ghost**; which is a new birth into righteousness; which is a change from darkness to light; from the power of Satan unto **God**.

This: blessed salvation that **God** hath made for us through the Blood of His Son was designed to free you from all the powers of Satan and make you heirs and joint heirs with **Christ**. O this blessed salvation; O this glorious inheritance that we have in **Jesus Christ**. It is a lovely thought to me. Three times **God** rent the heavens with the words, **"This is My Beloved Son, in whom I am well pleased."**

It is true that He was born in Bethlehem. It is true He worked with His father as a carpenter; it is true that there was evidence of a human order about Him; it is true, my brother, He was flesh like you and me; But it is also true that **God** dwelt in that flesh, and manifested His glory so that He overcame every temptation and trial of the devil! **1 Timothy 3:16 And without controversy great is the mystery of godliness: God was manifest in the flesh, justified in the Spirit, seen of angels, preached unto the Gentiles, believed on in the world, received up into glory.**

Smith Wigglesworth - JOY Unspeakable and Full of Glory

He kept the law and fulfilled His commission, so that He redeemed us by laying down His life. Glory to **God**! **Jesus** was "manifested in the flesh"; **"manifested to destroy the power of the devil."** What does that mean? It means this: that He was **God**'s perfect will in the flesh. O it is lovely!

I do not know anything more beautiful in the Bible than this example of **God**'s life and power.
What He did for and in **Jesus** He wants to do for, and in us. He can make us overcomers; destroying the power and the passion of the sinful nature; dwelling in us by His mighty power; to so transform our lives until we **love righteousness and hated iniquity**, and till we become **Holy** as he is **Holy**, because, as He **(God)** dwelt in His Son **Jesus** by the power of the **Holy Spirit**, so **God** can dwell in us. **"In His Son."**

O this blessed **Jesus**, the Son of **God, Who loved me and gave Himself for me.** This blessed, blessed Son of **God**. I want you to see that we receive sonship because of **His obedience**; because of **His loyalty**; and do not forget what the Scripture says: **"He learned obedience through the things he suffered."**

If you turn to the Scripture you will discover (as incredible as this may sound) that His whole kindred, His mother, brothers, sisters, and the rest of his kindred came and said, **"He is possessed by Beelzebub the devil, and is doing his works."**
See how **Jesus** suffered. They reviled Him and they tried to kill Him by throwing Him over the cliff, but **Jesus**

passed through the midst of the whole crowd, and as soon as He was escaped He saw a blind man and healed him as He was going on his Fathers way.

O it is lovely. He is **God**'s example of what can be, and I want to tell you all the attributes and the divine positions and the beatitudes that **Jesus** had. **He was in the world, but not of it**. O it is lovely; it is divinely glorious; and this power of the new creation, this birth unto righteousness by faith in the atonement, can so transform and change you that you can be just like **Jesus Christ**. You can know without a shadow of a doubt that it is Gods power dominating, controlling and filling you and making you like **Jesus**! Understand that though you are still in the body you can be governed by the **Spirit**.

What a **Holy** life! What a zeal! What a passion! 0, to live in all the beauties of all the glory and magnificent of the **Holy Ghost**! **Jesus** was truly the first fruits for us. O, the fascination of the **Christ** of **God** makes me realize there is nothing in this world worth grasping, worth having compared to him. O **Lord**, reveal yourself unto your people. I could never believe it was possible for any man to stand here and preach as I have preached if it was not real to me. I would be ashamed of myself if I did so. But it is not possible.

Beloved, it is the reality of **Christ** that constrains us. There is a constraining power in this blessed **Jesus Christ** of **God** which makes us know that there is something in it that is different from anything in the whole world. It is called in the Scriptures an **"unfeigned love."** It is a tremendously deep word: **"unfeigned love**

62

Smith Wigglesworth - JOY Unspeakable and Full of Glory

and faith." Whatever is it?

O beloved, He will tell you what it is. It is a complete denunciation of yourself as the power of **Christ** takes a hold of you, and you feel it would be death to grieve the heart of **God**. You love **God** so deeply that you could stand fire, water or anything in the way of persecution. **He loved you when you were yet sinners, and He seeks your love in return.** It is an unfeigned love, a love that can stand ridicule, persecution and slander, because it is a love that is in you by the power of the **Holy Ghost**. He is making you to know that **God** is changing you by His **Spirit** from one state of glory to another state of Glory in the **Holy Ghost**.

I am not at all surprised at His face shining; it is no wonder at the presence of **God** appearing on the Mount, It is no wonder of anything which glorifies the **Christ** of **God**, Who would deny Himself of life to save those of us that were lost in our sins and iniquity. O what a **Christ**! When we were enemies to Him He died for us! See this very moment that **Jesus** had opportunities which were offered to no other human soul in the world. It was not only the glory of **God** that was offered Him, but the manifestation of a human glory, the offer of which reached Him in the world, for they longed in certain circles to make Him a King.

O, if there was anybody in the world, out of all the countries and nations who was longing to make you a King, you would lose your head and you're commonsense and everything you have to be that king; but our blessed **Christ** of **God** walked away from them, and went to secluded prayer. He was the greatest King that ever the world will know. **He is King of Kings and Lord of Lords.** 0 yes, and of **His KINGDOM there shall be no end, and He shall see His seed; He shall prolong His days, and the pleasure of the Lord shall prosper in His hands.**

I wonder if there is any of the seed of the **Lord Jesus** in this place. 0 you that believe you are the seed of the Son of **God** through faith in Gods promise. The seed of the Son of **God**, by faith in **Christ**. The seed of the Son of **God** because His seed is in you, which is the Word of **God**, and you are saved by His power. All the seed in this place, let us see your hands. He shall see His seed; He shall prolong His days, and the pleasure of the **Lord** shall prosper in His hands. O **Hallellujah**!

Tongues and Interpretation of Same. "Glory to **God**! The living shall praise Him, for out of the dust He has brought forth a living harvest of souls to praise Him for eternity. He is seeing His seed, and the pleasure of the **Lord** is already prospering in His hands."

O beloved, this is the day of the visitation of the **Lord**. O what a **Christ** we have to-night! I want you all to see there is nothing like Him. If you see Him to-night, you needy ones, you sinners, as you gaze at Him you will be changed; as you look at Him you will find that your natural body will change; a strength will come to you; there is life in every look that you put on the Son of **God**: a perfect transformation in looking at Him. They saw Him transfigured. What a **Wonderful** transfiguring it was. O my dear friends, I want you to-night to see that

Smith Wigglesworth - JOY Unspeakable and Full of Glory

there was something else in it besides.

It was certainly a **Wonderful** place of transfiguration, for the disciples to see the KINGDOM of **God**. But what was it to **Jesus**? Our **God** is the **God** of the living! **Hallellujah**! And they that begin to live will never die; that is, in truth; and I do thank **God**,; because He is the **God** of Abraham, and Isaac and Jacob, and I love the fact of Him calling Himself the **God** of Jacob more than anything.

I know that if He was only the **God** of Abraham and Isaac, who was the seed of all future and eternal seed, we might have looked and said, "Who can reach Abraham's standard?" And we might have looked at Isaac, for there does not seem to be a flaw in Isaac; but when He says He is the **God** of Jacob, then there is room for everybody. O it is so lovely!

There is not a man in the world, and there is not a man at any time in human history, millionaires who could beat Jacob in his manipulation of gaining wealth—I tell you Jacob was equal to any of them?

There was not a thing that Jacob could not manipulate. It didn't matter how Laban came and made bargains with Jacob, Jacob was always the master. **Hallellujah**!

Is He your **God**? He is the **God** of the sinner. O, there is something **Wonderful** about these realities. He is the **God** of the helpless. He is full of mercy. I tell you He is your **God** and He is prepared to meet you exactly as He met Jacob. For Jacob had deceived in every way. He had deceived to get his birth-right; to get his cattle. He was a deceiver. Truly, the devil had a big part with Jacobs's life, but, praise **God**, there was one thing that Jacob knew, and that was this: He knew that **God** had fulfilled His promise.

There in Bethel **God** let him see the ladder, and it was a **Wonderful** ladder, for it reached from earth to heaven and he saw angels ascending, and descending. I am **Glad** that they began at the bottom of the ladder and went to the top. It was a lovely ladder I tell you, if they could begin at the bottom and go to the top. Bethel—the place of prayer; the place of changing conditions; earthy entering into the heavenly.

God brought Jacob right back to this same place. It did not matter how he had wandered; it didn't matter to **God**; it made no difference. **God** swore to him, and He brought him back; but he says, "O, my cattle are no good, my children are no good, my wives are no good, and the commandments are no good, because if Esau doesn't forgive me he will cut off my head.

The first thing, Jacob did is he let his cattle go over. What were cattle? **Nothing—to him**. Then he sent his servants, and then he let Leah go. But it was difficult to let Rachel go. But he had to let her go, and then he was alone in that **Holy** place. Then the same old Jacob was left, and as long as **God** would let him wrestle with Him he wrestled.

That is a type of holding on to this world—we never let go till we are obliged to. And **God** touched him, and as

Smith Wigglesworth - JOY Unspeakable and Full of Glory

soon as he was touched (and **God** has a way to touch us) he found out he was no good to himself or any one for that matter; then he cried out and said**, "Let me go,"** the angel said. But Jacob said, **"Don't go till you have blessed me."**

O brother, **God** will bless you if you get to this place of surrender. But you are no good as long as you are still wrestling for the things of this world; but when you come to a place of helplessness, a real cry of brokenness, then **God** will meet you. O, it is lovely—it is marvelous how **God** meets us in our distresses; when the cry comes from our broken hearts, then **God** comes. Have you been there yet?

How many times have you tried and failed? O my brother, let **God** come and bring your life to this glorious end, so the new man can come forth!

Let God come! Will you? O, it is so lovely to me to know that **God** in His mercy never fails. And when **Jesus** was there on the Mount in the glory, there came Moses and Elias speaking to **Jesus** about our salvation, talking to Him about His decease and His death at Jerusalem.

And when He came down from the Mount of Transfiguration, He set His face like a flint to fulfil his commission of pain and suffering for you and me. From the glory right to the Cross. Is this not a strange and **Wonderful** thing?

What a **Wonderful Jesus** we have! Hear what the Scripture says: "He came down from the mountain into the valley, and there was a man there which had a son, whom a devil had taken and thrown down and tormented." Did you ever read the tenth chapter of John? What does it say? **"The devil—the thief— cometh to steal, to kill and to destroy; but I have come to give life and life more abundant."** O **Hallellujah**! The thief cometh; but don't you see the thief cometh to destroy you; but **Jesus** came to give you life and life more abundantly.

And when **Jesus** came down amongst the crowd this man cried out and said, "Help me, **Lord**, help me. Here is my son; the devil taketh him and teareth him till he foams at the mouth, and there he lies prostrate. I brought him to your disciples, but they could not help me."

O brothers, **God** strengthen our hands, take away our unbelief and doubts. **Jesus said, "O faithless generation—how long must I suffer you? Bring him unto Me." And they brought him to Jesus, and Jesus cast out the evil Spirit.** Do you know that even in the presence of **Jesus Christ** these evil spirits tore the boy and left him as one dead? Just think about satanic powers. He goeth about to kill; seeking whom he may devour. May **God** save us and keep us in the place where the devil shall have no power and no victory over us. He is come; but our **Lord** is come.

Bless the Name of **Jesus**; has He come to you? He wants to come to you. He wants to be involved in your whole life. Nay, verily He wants to transform your life through His power this very day, and I pray **God** that the demon powers which come out of everyone to-night shall never

Smith Wigglesworth - JOY Unspeakable and Full of Glory

get back in again. Oh, if I could only speak so as to show you what it means to be delivered by the power of **Jesus Christ**, and what it means when you lose your deliverance through your own stupidity and folly. There was a case like this; a man, possessed with demon power and sickness and every weakness came to **Jesus** and **Jesus** cast the evil spirits out, and the man was made whole.

Then, instead of the man seeking the **Holy Spirit** and the light of **God** he began to walk the same old ways. We need to be like blind Bartimaeus who walked with **Jesus** after he was healed. But instead of that, he went afterwards to the first race meeting there was. **God** save us. The healing power is for the glory of **God**, and it appears that this man was swept and garnished, and the evil **Spirit** had nowhere to go, and went to the Savior to see if they could gain an entrance once again into him, and they went back and found the man was not inhabited with a love for the truth!

He had not been filled with **Christ** and the power of the **Spirit**, and so they entered into that man and his case was worse than before. If you want healing by the power of **God** it means your lives have to be filled with **God**. Will it last? Get **Jesus** on board and it lasts forever. You cannot keep yourself. No man is capable of standing against the wiles of the devil by himself, but when you get **Jesus** in you will be equal to a million devils.

We must not only be swept and garnished, but must see that the power and truth of **God** comes to inhabit us. What are you going to do with this position? None is safe without **Christ**. The weak man is capable if he is in **Christ Jesus**. Are you willing to so surrender yourself to **God** this moment that Satan shall have no dominion over you? In the name of **Jesus**, I pray you are?

The power of God is just the same to-day.
It doesn't matter what the people say,
Whatever God has promised He is able to perform,
For the power of God is just the same to-day.

(15) MORE QUOTES

SMITH WIGGLESWORTH

"When the saint ceases to seek after holiness, purity, righteousness, truth; when he ceases to pray, stops reading the Word and gives way to carnal appetites, then it is that Satan comes."

"Faith is just the open door through which the Lord comes. Do not say, 'I was saved by faith' or 'I was healed by faith.' Faith does not save and heal. God saves and heals through that open door. You believe, and the power of Christ comes."

"The resurrected **Christ** is there for you. Trust His presence. Trust His power. Trust His provision. He is alive for you!"

"We have a big God. We have a Wonderful Jesus. We have a glorious Comforter. God's canopy is over you and will cover you at all times, preserving you from evil. Under His wings shalt thou trust. The Word of God is living and powerful and in its treasures you will find eternal life. If you dare trust this Wonderful Lord, the Lord of life, you will find in Him everything you need."

"There is a place where **God**, through the power of the **Holy Ghost**, reigns supreme in our lives."

"**The power of God is beyond all our conception. The trouble is that we do not have the power of God in a full manifestation because of our finite thoughts, but as we go on and let God have His way, there is no limit to what our limitless God will do in response to a limitless faith. But you will never get anywhere except you are in constant pursuit of all the life of God.**"

It was His purpose to die for the world. Oh dear saint, will it ever be spoken thru your lips or your mind that you will ever have a desire to serve **Christ** like that? Will you and I, under every circumstances take up your cross so fully, to be in the place of any ridicule, any surrender?

"**The power of God will take you out of your own plans and put you into the plan of God.**"

"**God** has something better for you than you have ever had in the past. Come out into all the fullness of faith and power and life and victory that He is willing to provide, as you forget the things of the past, and press right on for the prize of His calling in **Christ Jesus**."

"Hard things are always opportunities to gain more glory for the **Lord** as He manifests His power. Every trial is a blessing. … The hardest things are simply lifting places into the grace of **God**."

"We have a Wonderful God, a God whose ways are past finding out, and whose grace and power are limitless."

"Repeat in your heart often **"baptized with the Holy Ghost and fire, fire, fire!"** All the unction, and weeping, and travailing comes through the baptism of fire, and I say to you and say to myself, purged and cleansed and filled with renewed spiritual power." "Who maketh his ministers a flame of fire." Heb. 1:7

"God has never changed the order of things: first there comes the natural, and then the spiritual. For instance, when it is on your heart to pray, you begin in the natural and your second word will probably be under the power of the Spirit. You begin and God will end.

It is the same in giving forth utterances under the Spirit's power. You feel the moving of the Spirit within and you begin to speak and the Spirit of God will give forth utterance. Thousands have missed Wonderful blessings because they have not had faith to move out and begin in the natural, in faith that the Lord would take them into the realm of the supernatural. When you receive the Holy Ghost you receive God's Gift, in whom are all the gifts of the Spirit."

"It is an insult to ask **God** for power after you have received the baptism of the **Holy Ghost**. You have power! But you have to ACT!

*I see more and more in this glorious life of God, that there is a

Smith Wigglesworth - JOY Unspeakable and Full of Glory

pure whiteness to be achieved, there is a pure son ship without fear and the saints of God shall rise in such confidence until they will remove what people think are mountains, till they will subdue what you call KINGDOMs.

The Loveliest

The power of the **Holy Spirit** is the loveliest, and divine in all of his construction. He is a great refiner. He is full of life, but it is always divine—never natural. If you deal in the flesh after you are baptized in the **Holy Spirit**, you cease to go deeper.

Beloved, I want to speak about something greater; something to lift your minds, elevate your thoughts, and bring you into deep and divine ways; something that elevates you out of yourself and into **God**, out of the world and into a place where you know you have rest for your feet, where you cease from your own works (Heb. 4:10), and where **God** works in you mightily *"to will and to do for His good pleasure"* (Phil. 2:13).

When I think about a river—a pure, **Holy**, divine river—I say, "What can stand against its mighty rush?" Wherever it is—in a railway coach, in the street, or in a meeting—its power and flow will always be felt; it will always do its work. **Jesus** spoke about the **Holy Spirit** that was to be given. I want you to think about how **God** gave him, how his coming was manifested, and his reception and his outflow after he had come."

CHAPTER FIVE
Receive the Power of the Holy Spirit

"I know it was personally right, it was divinely right, for those apostles to hear what **Jesus** said and to tarry for the **Holy Spirit**; however, it is longer right to tarry for the **Holy Spirit**. **Then why do we not all receive the Power of the Holy Spirit, you ask?** Because our bodies are not ready for it; our temples are not cleansed.

When our temples are purified, and our minds are put in order, so that carnalities and fleshly desires, and everything contrary to the **Spirit** have gone, then the **Holy Spirit can take full charge**. The **Holy Spirit** is not a manifestation of carnality. There are any number of people who never read the Word of **God** and who are easily led away by the powers of Satan.

Smith Wigglesworth - JOY Unspeakable and Full of Glory

After ye have received power

The word of **God** is **Wonderful** and I believe that **God** wants to fill us with his word. He wants us to be so filled with it that no matter where we are, the word will be lived out in us. The word is power, the word is life, the word of **God** is faith, the word is **Jesus** and the word of **God** is everlasting life to him that believeth.

"He that [hath] my word, and believeth on him that sent me, hath everlasting life." [Jn 5.24]

We need to be careful in reading the word; I believe it is too precious to rush over; we have need to **"rightly [divide] the word of truth." [2Ti 2.15]** I want to speak to you about the power given by **God**. Oh the power of the **Holy Ghost**! The power that quickens, the revealing power, the travailing power! The power that lives and moves! The power that brings about exactly what **Jesus** said, **"When you receive… ye shall have power." [Ac 1.8, para.]**

One day as I came into the house my wife said, "Which way did you come into the house?" I answered that I had come in by the back way. "Oh," she said. "If you had come in by the front you would have seen a man there in a terrible state. There is a crowd of people around him and he is in terrible straits." Then the doorbell rang and she said, "There he is again. What will we do?" I said, "Just be quiet and still." I rushed to the door and just as I was opening it the **Spirit** said, **"This is what I baptized**

you for."

I was very careful then in opening the door, and then I heard the man crying outside, "Oh I have committed the unpardonable sin; I am lost, I am lost." I asked him to come in and when he got inside he said again in awful distress, "I am lost, I am lost." Then the **Spirit** came upon me and **I commanded the lying Spirit to come out of the man in the name of Jesus.** Suddenly he lifted up his arms and said, "I never did it." The moment that the lying **Spirit** was out of him he was able to speak the truth. It was at that very moment that I realized the power that is in the baptism of the **Holy Spirit**. It was the **Spirit** that said, **"This is what I baptized you for,"** and I believe we ought to be in the place where we will always be able to understand the mind of the **Spirit** amidst all the other voices in the world.

After the **Holy Ghost** has come upon you, you have power. I believe a great mistake is made in these days by people tarrying and tarrying after they have received. After you have received it is, **"Go ye."** Not "sit still," but **"Go ye into all the world, and preach the gospel."** **[Mk 16.15]** We will be in terrible havoc if (by unbelief) turn back again and cry out to **God** seeking something we already have. I want you to see that **God** is depending upon us in these last days. Also there is no room for anyone to boast, and the man who goes about saying, **"Look at me for I am somebody,"** is of no value whatever to the KINGDOM. **God** will not be able to use such a fellow to any great degree! **God** will have a people to glorify him. Granted **God** is doing what he can with that which he has, but we are so unwilling at times

Smith Wigglesworth - JOY Unspeakable and Full of Glory

to move into the plan of **God** that He has to chastise us many times to get us where he can use us.

Jesus was so filled with the **Holy Ghost** that he lived in the place where he was always ready to act upon His Fathers Voice. He was always in the attitude where he could bring victory out of every opportunity. The power of the **Holy Spirit** is within us but it can only be manifested as we go in obedience to that opportunity which we have before us. I believe if you wait until you think you have power after you have received the **Holy Ghost** you will never know you have it.

Don't you know that the child of **God** who is in possession of the baptism is inhabited by the power of the **Spirit**? You will remember one time when they tried to throw **Jesus** from the brow of the hill, [Lk 4.29] that he passed through the midst of them. As soon as he got free from them he healed a man with blind eyes. Pressing through the crowd which was trying to kill him, he showed forth his power by healing this blind man. Some people might think that **Jesus** should have run away altogether but he stopped to heal. This thought has comforted me over and over through the years.

One day as I was waiting for a car I stepped into a shoemaker's shop. I had not been there long when I saw a man with a green shade over his eyes, crying pitifully and in great agony. It was heartrending and the shoemaker told me that the inflammation was destroying his eyes. I jumped up and went to the man and said, **"You devil, come out of this man in the name of Jesus."** Instantly the man said, "It is all gone, I can see now." That is the only scriptural way, to begin to work at once, and preach afterwards. You will find as the days go by that miracles and healings will be manifested as act upon the quickening of Gods **Spirit**! Because the Master was touched with the feeling of the infirmities of the multitudes they instantly gathered around him to hear what He had to say concerning the word of **God**.

However, I would rather see one man saved than ten thousand people healed. If you ask me why, I would call to your attention the word which says, **"There was a [rich man and he] fared sumptuously every day." [Lk 16.19]** Now we don't hear of this man having any diseases but it says, **"In hell he lift up his eyes." [Lk 16.23]** We also read that there was a poor man full of sores **[Lk 16.20]** and **"he lifted up his eyes in heaven,"** so we see that a man can die practically in good health but be lost, and a man can die in disease and be saved; so it is more important to be saved than anything else.

But **Jesus** was sent to bear the infirmities and the afflictions of the people and to destroy the works of the devil. He said that the thief (which is the devil) **cometh to steal and to kill and to destroy, but "I am come that [ye] might have life, and have it more abundantly." [Jn 10.10]** I maintain that **God** wishes all his people to have this (ZOE) life more abundant; that if we understood sin as we ought to understand it and realized that there is no sickness without disobedience, ignorance of Gods will, or lack of Faith! You will say that this is rather strong, but we have the remedy in the **word of God**! **Jesus** paid the full price and the full redemption for every need, and where sin abounded, grace can come in

Smith Wigglesworth - JOY Unspeakable and Full of Glory

and much more abound, **[Ro 5.20]** and dispel all the sickness.

When I was traveling from England to Australia on January 6th I witnessed for **Jesus**, and it was not long before I had plenty of room to myself. If you want a whole seat to yourself just begin to **preach Jesus**. However, some people listened and began to be much affected. One of the young men said to me, "I have never heard these truths before. You have so moved me that I must have a deeper conversation with you."

 The young man told me that his wife was a great believer in Christian Science but was very sick. And although she had tried everything she had been unable to get relief; she had hired a personal doctor, but the doctor gave her no hope whatever. and in her terrible dilemma and facing the realities of death, she asked that she might have an appointment with the man in second class who was preaching, because, she said, "the things he says makes us feel he is for real." So they made an appointment and when I got to her I felt it would be unwise to say anything about Christian Science, so I just said, "You are in bad shape." She said, "Yes, they give me no hope."

I said, "I will not speak to you about anything but will just lay my hands upon you in the **name of Jesus**, and **when I do you will be healed." Christ** healed her instantly. That woke her up spiritually and she began to think seriously about **God**. For three days she was lamenting over the things she might have to give up. "Will I have to give up the cigarettes?" "No," I said.

"Will I have to give up the dance?" and again I replied "No." "Well, we have a little drinking sometimes and then we play cards also. Will I have to give—?" "No," I said, "you will not have to give up anything. **Only let us see Jesus.**"

And right then she got such a vision of her **crucified savior**, and **Jesus was made so real** to her that she at once told her friends that she could not play cards any more, could not drink or dance any more, and she said she would have to go back to England to preach against this awful thing, Christian Science. Oh, what a revelation **Jesus** gave her! Now if I had refused to go when called for, saying that I first had to go to my cabin and pray about it, the **Lord** might have let that opportunity slip by. After you have received the **Holy Ghost** you have power; you don't have to wait.

The other day we were going through a very thickly populated part of San Francisco when we noticed a large crowd gathered. I saw it from the window of the car and said I had to get out, which I did. There in the midst was **a boy in the agonies of death**. As I threw my arms around the boy I asked what the trouble was and he answered that he had cramps. In the name of **Jesus** I commanded the devils to come out of him and at once he jumped up, and not even taking time to thank me, ran off perfectly healed. We are **God**'s own children, quickened by his **Spirit** and he has given us power over all the powers of darkness; **Christ** in us the open evidence of eternal glory, **Christ** in us the life, the truth and the way.

We have a **Wonderful** salvation that is available for

Smith Wigglesworth - JOY Unspeakable and Full of Glory

everybody. I believe that most baptized people have no conception of the true power **God** has given them until they realize what they have. I maintain that Peter and John had no true idea of the greatness of the power they had, but they began to see it. They said, **"Well, as far as money goes, we have none of that, but we do have something; we don't exactly know what it is, but we will try it on you. In the name of Jesus of Nazareth, rise up and walk,"** **[Ac 3.6, para]** and it worked. In order to make yourself realize what you have in your possession you will have to try it and I can assure you it will work. I said one time to a man that the Acts of the Apostles would never have been written if the Apostles had not acted, and the **Holy Spirit** is still continuing his acts through us.

May **God** help us to step into theses amazing acts. There is nothing like Pentecost and if you have never been baptized in the **Holy Ghost**, you are making a big mistake by waiting. Don't you know that the only purpose for which **God** saved you was that you might be a savior of others? And for you to think that you are to remain stationary and just get to heaven is a great mistake. **The baptism is to make you a witness for Jesus.** Thank **God** the hardest way is the best way; you never hear anything about the person who is always having an easy time. The preachers always tell of how Moses crossed the Red Sea when he was at wits' end. I cannot find the record of anyone in the scriptures whom **God** used who was not first tried. So if you never have any trials it is because you are not worthy of them.

God wants us to walk power. When I was traveling in

Sweden at a certain train station early in the morning a little lady and her daughter got onto the train. I saw at once that the lady was in dreadful agony and asked my interpreter to inquire as to her trouble. With tears running down her face she told us how her daughter was taking her to the hospital to have her legs amputated.

Everything that was possible had been done for her. I told her **Jesus** could heal. Just then the train stopped and a crowd of people entered until there was hardly standing room, but friends, we never get into a place that is too awkward for **God**, though it seemed to me that the devil had sent these people in at that time to hinder. However, when the train began to move along I got down, although it was terribly crowded, and put my hands upon the woman's leg I prayed for her in the name of **Jesus**. At once she said to her daughter, **"I am healed.**

My leg is all better now; I felt power go down my leg," and she began to walk about at that very moment. When the train stopped at the next station and this woman got out and walked up and down the platform; saying, **"I am healed. I am healed."** **Jesus** was the first fruits, and **God** has chosen us in **Christ** and has revealed his Son in us that we might manifest him in power. **God** gives us power over the devil and when we say the devil we mean everything that is wicked and not of **God**. Some people say we can afford to do without the baptism of the **Holy Ghost** but I say we cannot. I believe any person who thinks there is a stop between Calvary and the glory has made a big mistake

Smith Wigglesworth - JOY Unspeakable and Full of Glory

The KINGDOM of Heaven

When Satan entered into Judas, the only people that the devil could speak to thru Judas were the priests, sad as it is to say. They conspired to get Judas to betray **Jesus**, and the devil used money from these priests to put **Jesus** to death. Now it is a very serious thing, for we must clearly understand whether we are of the right **Spirit** or not, for no man can be of the **Spirit** of **Christ** and persecute another. No man can have the true **Spirit** of **Jesus Christ** and slay his brother, and no man can follow the **Lord Jesus** and have hate in his heart. You cannot have **Jesus** and have bitterness and hatred, and persecute other believers.

It is possible for us, if we are not careful, to have within us an evil **Spirit** of unbelief, and even in our best state it is possible for us to have bitterness unless we are perfectly dead to self and let the life of the **Lord** lead and guide us. You remember **Jesus** wanted to pass thru a certain place as He was going to Jerusalem, because He would not stop and preach to them concerning the KINGDOM, but they refused to allow Him to go thru their section of the country. And the disciples which were with **Jesus** said to Him, **"Shall we call down fire from heaven upon them as Elijah did?"** But **Jesus** turned and said**, "Ye know not what Spirit ye are of."**

There they were, following **Jesus** and with Him all the time, but **Jesus** rebuked that **Spirit**. I pray **God** that we may give us understanding of this truth in this service. That our knowledge of **Jesus** is pure love, and pure love to **Jesus** is death to self on all areas, body, soul and **Spirit**. I believe if we are in the will of **God**, we will be perfectly influenced at all times, and if we would know anything about the mighty works of **Christ**, we shall have to follow what **Jesus** preached. Whatever He said came to pass.

Many things happened in the lives of the apostles to show the power of **Christ** over all flesh. In regard to paying tribute, **Jesus** said to Peter, "We are free, we can enter into the city without paying tribute; nevertheless, we will pay." I like that thought, that **Jesus** was so righteous on all situations. It helps me tremendously. Then **Jesus** told Peter to do a very hard thing. He said, **"Take that hook and cast it into the sea.**

Draw out a fish and take from its gills a piece of silver for thee and Me." This was one of the hardest things Peter had to do. He had been fishing all his life, but never had he taken silver out of a fish's mouth. There were thousands and millions of fish in the sea, but one fish had to have a piece of silver in it. He went down to the sea as any natural man would, speculating and thinking, "How can it be?" But how could it not be, if **Jesus** said it would be? Then the perplexity would arise, "But how many fish

Smith Wigglesworth - JOY Unspeakable and Full of Glory

there are, and which fish has the money?" Brother, if **God** speaks, it will be as He says.

What you need is to know the mind of **God** and the Word of **God**, and you will be so free you will never find a frown on your face, nor a tear in your eye of unbelief again. The more you know of the mightiness of the revelation of **God**, the more everything in the way of fearfulness pass away.

To know **God**, is to be in the place of triumph. To know **God** is to be in the place of rest. To know **God** is to be in the place of absolute victory. No doubt many things were in Peter's mind that day, but thank **God** there was one fish, and he obeyed. Sometimes to obey in blindness brings the victory. Sometimes when perplexities arise in your mind, obedience means **God** working out the problem. Peter cast the hook into the sea, and it would have been amazing if you could have seen the disturbance the other fish made to move out of the way, all excepting the right one. Just one among the millions of fish **God** wanted. **God** may put his hand upon you in the midst of millions of people, but if He speaks to you, that thing that He says will come to pass.

On this occasion, **Jesus** said to Peter and the rest, that when they went out into the city they would see a man bearing a pitcher of water, and they should follow him. It was not customary in the East for men to carry anything on their heads. The women always did the carrying, but this had to be a man, and he had to have a pitcher. One day there was a man preaching and he said it was quite all right for **Jesus** to go and arrange, for a colt to be tied there, and another preacher said it was quite easy to feed all those thousands of people, because the loaves in those days were so tremendously big, but he didn't tell them it was a little boy that had the five loaves. Unbelief can be very blind, but faith can see thru a stone-wall. Faith when it is moved by the power of **God** can laugh at every adversity.

They said to the man with the pitcher, "Where is the guest chamber?" "How strange it is that you should ask," he replied, "I have been preparing that, wondering who wanted it." It is marvelous when **God** is leading how perfectly everything works into the plan. He was arranging everything. You think He cannot do that today for you? People who have been in perplexities for days and days, He knows how to deliver out of trouble; He knows how to be with you in the dark hour.

He can make all things work together for good to them that love **God**. He has a way of arranging His plan, and when **God** comes in, you always know it was a day you lived in **God**. Oh to live in **God**! There is a vast difference between living in **God** and living in speculation and hope. There is something better than hope; something better than speculation. **"They that know their God shall be strong and do exploits,"** and **God** would have us to know Him.

Smith Wigglesworth - JOY Unspeakable and Full of Glory

"And when the hour was come, He sat down and the twelve apostles with Him." "When the hour was come". That was the most **Wonderful** hour these men had ever experienced. There never was an hour, never will be an hour like that hour on earth again. What hour was it? It was an hour of the passing of creation under the blood. It was an hour of destruction of demon power. It was an hour appointed of life coming out of death. It was an hour when all that ever lived came under a glorious covering and cleansing of the blood of **Christ**.

It was an hour when all the world was coming into emancipation by the blood of **God**. It was an hour in the world's history when it emerged from dark chaos, a **Wonderful** hour! Praise **God** for that hour! Was it a dark hour? It was a dark hour for Him, but a **Wonderful** light dawned for us. It was horribly dark for the Son of Man, but praise **God** He came thru it.

An Amazing and Wonderful Thought

There are some things in the Scriptures which move me greatly. I am **Glad** that Paul was a man. I am **Glad** that **Jesus** was a Man. I am **Glad** that Daniel was a man, and I am also **Glad** that John was a man. You ask Why? Because I see that whatever **God** has done for other men, He can do for me. And I find **God** has done such **Wonderful** things for other men that I am always acknowledging that these things are possible for me. Thinking about this is a **Wonderful** thought to me.

Jesus said in that dark and trying hour: **"I have a desire to eat this Passover with you before I suffer."** Desire? What could be His desire? His desire because of the salvation of the world. His desire because of the dethronement of the powers of Satan. His desire because He knew he was going to conquer all the works of the enemy and make every man free that ever lived. It was a great desire, but what lay between it? Just between that and his resurrection was the cross and Gethsemane! Some people say that **Jesus** died on the cross.

It is perfectly true, but is that the only place? **Jesus** died in Gethsemane. That was the tragic moment! That was the place where He paid the ultimate debt. It was in Gethsemane, and Gethsemane was between Him and the resurrection. He had a desire to eat this Passover and knew Gethsemane was between Him and the resurrection.

I want you to think about Gethsemane. There alone, and with the tremendous weight, the awful effect of all sin and disease upon his body, He cries out, **"If it be possible, let it pass."** Oh could it be! He could only save when He was man, but here in a great chaos of darkness He comes forth: **"To this end I came."**

It was His purpose to die for the world. Oh dear saint, will it ever be spoken thru your lips or your mind that you will ever have a desire to serve **Christ** like that? Will you and I, under every circumstances take up your cross

Smith Wigglesworth - JOY Unspeakable and Full of Glory

so fully, to be in the place of any ridicule, any surrender? **Jesus** desired to eat the Passover with His disciples, knowing what it meant?

It can only come out of the depths of love we have for Him that we can say this morning, **"Lord Jesus, I will follow."** Oh how very **Wonderful** is this decision in our heart! **God** knows the heart. You do not always have to be on the house-top to shout to indicate the condition of your heart. He knows your inward heart. You say, "I would be insanity not to be willing to suffer for **Jesus** when he so earnestly desired to suffer in order to save me." **"With desire,"** He says.

I know what it is to have the KINGDOM of heaven within you. He said that even the least in the KINGDOM of heaven is greater than John the Baptist, meaning those who are under the blood, those who have seen the **Lord** by faith, those who know by redemption they are made sons of **God**. I say to you, He will never taste again until we are there with Him. The KINGDOM will never be complete and it could not be fulfilled until we are all there at that great Supper of the Lamb where there will be millions and trillions of redeemed, which no man can number. We shall be there when that Supper is taking place. I like to think upon these realities.

I hope you will take a bold step into these truths with **God** and believe it. It is an act of faith **God** wants to bring you into; a perfecting of that love that cannot fail to accomplish **God**'s will. It is a fact that He has opened the KINGDOM of heaven to all believers, and that He gives eternal life to them that believe. The **Lord**, the Omnipotent **God**, it is He that knows the end from the beginning, and has arranged by the blood of the Lamb to clans the guilty and make intercession for all believers. Oh it is a **Wonderful** inheritance of faith to find shelter and forgiveness through the blood of **Jesus**!

I want you to see that He says, **"Do this in remembrance of Me."** He took the cup, He took the bread, and He gave thanks. The very attitude of giving thanks for His shed blood, giving thanks for His broken body, overwhelms the heart. To think that my **Lord** could give thanks for His shed blood which he is about to pour out for us! To think that my **Lord** could give thanks for His broken body which is about to be broken for us!

Only Almighty **God** can reveal this heroic act of **Jesus** to our human heart! The natural man cannot receive it, but the spiritual man, the man who has been created anew by faith in **Christ**, he is able to receive it. The man who believes **God** comes in into our hearts with the eternal seed of truth and righteousness and faith, and from the moment he sees the truth by faith he is made a new creation.

The flesh from that moment begins to wither, and the spiritual man begins take over. One begins to passes off, the other begins to passes on, until a man takes on the image and the likeness of **God**. I say the **Lord** brings a child of faith into a place of rest, and causes him to sit with **Christ** in heavenly places, giving him a language in the **Spirit** and making him know he no longer belongs to the law of sin and death.

You see this bread which represents His broken body? The **Lord** knew He could not bring us any nearer to His broken body. Our bodies are made of bread. The body of **Jesus** was made of that bread, and He knew He could bring us no nearer. He took the natural elements and said, "This bread represents my broken body." Now will it ever become that body of **Christ**? No, never. You cannot make it so. It is foolishness to believe it, but I take it as an emblem, and illustration and when I eat it, the natural leads me into the supernatural, and instantly I begin to feed on the supernatural by faith, One leads me into the other.

Jesus said, **"Take eat, this is my body."** I have a Revelation of knowledge of **Christ** thru this emblem, symbol. May we take from the table of the riches of His promises. The riches of heaven are before us. Fear not, only believe, for **God** has opened the treasures of His **Holy** Word.

The Perfection of JOY

Now if that same **Spirit** was in any church, it would purify the church. But I fear sometimes Satan gets the advantage and things are told before they are true. I believe **God** wants to so sanctify us, so separate us, that we will have that perfection of love that will not speak ill of a brother, that will not, slander a brother whether it is true or not.

There was strife among them who should be the greatest, but He said, **"He that is chief let him be as he that doth serve,"** and then he, the Master said, **"I am among you as one that serveth."** He, the noblest, the purest, the holiest, He was the servant of all! Exercising lordship over another is not of **God**. We must learn in our hearts that fellowship, true righteousness, loving one another and preferring one another must come into the church.

Jesus Wants All his People to be Free

I love to think that **Jesus** wants all his people to be full of His power, and that he wants all men to be overcomers. It is the **JOY God** brings within a human life that transforms it by his **word** and brings us into the place where we know it is above all opposition, and brings to naught the things that are, because **God** is in the **word**. Nothing but Gods power will do it.

Power over sin, power over sickness, power over the devil, power over all the powers of the devil! I know that

Smith Wigglesworth - JOY Unspeakable and Full of Glory

Jesus revealed by his word these truths—**"after that ye shall have power." [Ac 1.8, para.]** I think there is nothing more beautiful to experience are own personal Jordan River baptism.

The moment that **Jesus** was baptized in the **Holy Ghost** there was a manifestation that never appeared in the world before or since. Right there by the River Jordan was the Son of **God** baptized in the **Holy Ghost**. He came upon **Jesus** in the form of a dove. At that moment in the heavens above came the voice of **God**. [Lk 3.22] It is beautiful to think of how the Trinity is reaching out to humanity.

Why have we power when the **Holy Ghost** comes? Because the **Holy Ghost** reveals **Jesus**; and **Jesus** is the word of **God**. In that word there is all power. In order to understand what it means to have all power there are two things necessary; **#1** is to have ears to hear and **#2** is to have hearts to receive it.

I am sure that everyone should know this truth that **God** sent the devil out of heaven because he was evil; if he had been **Holy** he would not have sent him out. You never find anything that is impure get purer, but always viler, and Satan when he was cast out became weaker, viler, and more impure. Every born saint of **God**, filled with the **Spirit**, has a real revelation of that truth, **"Greater is he that is in you, than he that is in the world." [1Jn 4.4]** I say this with as much audacity as I can.

I know evil spirits are in abundance and in multitudes beyond count; **Jesus** cast them out as a legion. Satan and his angels were cast out of heaven and it seems to me that Satan had power to make evil spirits, but these are never as strong as Satan himself. Because of purity, holiness and righteousness, they that are strong shall become more and more righteous, and equally so. Satan and his emissaries become viler and viler, but also weaker and weaker.

But the believer because of the **Spirit** that is in him has the **power to cast out these evil spirits**. It must be so; **God** wants us to have this power operating in us; **we must be able to destroy Satan's power wherever we go.**

When I received the **Holy Ghost** all the people thought that I had lost my mind, but we have to live a life that gives evidence to the presence of the **Holy Spirit**. It is a strange fact but people who are of this world seem to be in a terrible condition and they honestly do not know what to do.

COME OUT OF THEM

For years and years **God** has been making me appear to hundreds and thousands of people as a fool. I remember the day when He saved me and when He called me out. If there is a thing **God** wants to do today He wants to be as real to you and me as He was to Abraham. After I was saved I joined myself up to a very lively group of people

Smith Wigglesworth - JOY Unspeakable and Full of Glory

who were full of a **Spirit** of revival, and it was marvelous how **God** blest this gathering of believers. But then there came a Luke warmness and indifference amongst us, and **God** said to me as clearly as anything, **"Come out."**

I obeyed and came out. The people said, "We cannot understand you. We need you now and you are leaving us." The Plymouth Brethren at that time were in a Conference. The Word of **God** was with them in power, the love of **God** was with them. Baptism by immersion was revealed to me, and when my friends saw me go into the water they said I was altogether wrong. But **God** had called me and I obeyed. The day came when I saw that the Brethren had dropped down to the letter, all letter, dry and barren.

At that time the Salvation Army was filled with love, filled with power, filled with zeal; every place a revival, and I joined up with them. For about six years the glory of **God** was there, and then the **Lord** said again, **"Come out,"** and I am **Glad** I came. The Salvation Army became a social movement and **God** has no place for a social movement. We are saved by regeneration, from glory to glory and the man who is going deeper with **God** has no time for social reforms.

God moved on, and at that time there were many people who were receiving the baptism of the **Holy Ghost** without signs. Those days were **"days of heaven on earth."** **God** unfolded the truth, showed the way of sanctification by the power of the blood of **Jesus Christ**, and I experienced the great inflow of the life of **God**. I thank **God** for that, but **God** came along again and said, **"Come out."** I obeyed **God** and went with what they called the "tongues" people; they had further light that I needed. I saw **God** advancing every step I made, and I can see even in this Pentecostal work, except we see there is a real death yourself, **God** will say to us, **"Come out."**

Unless the present Pentecost movement wakes up to shake herself free from all carnal worldly things and comes into a place of the divine-likeness with **God**, we will hear the voice of **God** once again say, **"Come out"** and He will give us something far better than what we now have.

I ask every one of you listening to the sound of my voice, will you hear the **voice of God** and come out? You ask, **"What do you mean?"** Everyone who is hungry for **God** knows without exception, there is only one word for Pentecost, and that is FIRE! If you are not on fire you are not in the place were **God** can mightily use you. It is only the FIRE of **God** that burns up the entanglements of the world.

When we came into this new work **God** spoke to us by the **Spirit** and we knew we had to reach the place of absolute submission and cleansing, so that there would be nothing left. We were swept and garnished. Now, that

Smith Wigglesworth - JOY Unspeakable and Full of Glory

was only the beginning, and if you have not made spiritual progress into that **Holy** place of zeal, power and COMPASSION for **God**, we can truly say you have backslidden in heart. The backslider in heart is dead to Gods fullness. He is not having the open vision. The backslider in heart is not seeing the Word of **God** living and fresh every day.

You can put it down that a man is a backslider in heart if does not hate the sinful things of the world. And if you have the applause of the world you do not having the approval of **God**. I do not know whether you will receive it or not but my heart burns with this message, "changing in the regeneration" for in this changing you will get a place in the KINGDOM to come where you shall be in authority; that place which **God** has prepared for us, that place which is beyond all human conception. We can catch a glimpse of that glory, when we see how John worshipped the angel, and the angel said to him**, "See thou do it not, for I am thy fellow-servant, of thy brethren the prophets."** This angel is showing John the wonders of the glorious KINGDOM and in his glorified state, John thought he was the **Lord**. I wonder if we dare believe for this glorious place.

Let me close with these words: As sure as we have borne the image of the earthly, we shall also have the image of the heavenly. It means to us that everything of an earthly type has to cease, for the heavenly type is so **Wonderful** in all of its purity. **God**, full of love, full of purity, full of power! No power only in the realm of purity! No open door into heaven only in the place of the conscience being void of sin between man and **God**, the heavens open only where the **Spirit** of the **Lord** is so leading, so that flesh has no power, but we will live in and by the **Spirit**. **God** bless you and prepare you for greater days

It is written of Christ, "Thou lovest righteousness, and hatest wickedness." And in this new life in the Spirit, in this new covenant life, you love the things that are right and pure and Holy, and shudder at all things that are wrong.

Jesus was able to say, "The prince of this world cometh, and bath nothing in Me," and the moment we are filled with the Spirit of God we are brought into like Wonderful condition, and, as we continue to be filled with the Spirit, the enemy cannot have an inch of territory in us.

This is the Day of Purifying

Seek the **Lord** and He will sanctify every thought, every act, till your whole being is ablaze with **Holy** purity and your one desire will be for Him who has created you in holiness. Oh, this holiness! Can we be made pure? We can. Every inbred sin must go. **God** can cleanse away every evil thought.

Smith Wigglesworth - JOY Unspeakable and Full of Glory

Can we have a hatred for sin and a love for righteousness? Yes, **God** will create within thee a pure heart. He will take away the stony heart out of the flesh. He will sprinkle thee with clean water and thou shalt be cleansed from all thy filthiness. When will He do it? When you seek Him for such inward purity.

This is the day of holiness. This is the day of separation. This is the day of waking. O **God**, let us wake today! Let the inner **Spirit** wake into consciousness that **God** is calling us. The **Lord** is upon us. We see that the day is upon us. We look at the left side, we look at the right side, we see everywhere new theories. New things will not stand the light of the truth When you see these, things, you know that there must be a great falling away before the day And it is coming. It is upon us.

*I hope you will take a bold step into these truths with God and believe it. It is an act of faith God wants to bring you into; a perfecting of that love that cannot fail to accomplish God's will. It is a fact that He has opened the KINGDOM of heaven to all believers, and that He gives eternal life to them that believe.

CHAPTER SIX

(25) QUOTES ON: OUR NEW LIFE

SMITH WIGGLESWORTH

*"Herein is my Father glorified, that ye bear much fruit ..." (John 15:8). He has no way in which to get fruit, only through us. We have not to be ordinary people.

 To be saved is to be an extraordinary man, an exposition of God. When Jesus was talking about the new life He said, "...Except a man be born again [of God], he cannot see the KINGDOM of God. That which is born of the flesh is flesh; and that which is"

God is Compassionate and says, **"Seek ye the Lord while he may be found." [Is 55.6]** And He has further stated, **"Whosoever shall call on the name of the Lord**

Smith Wigglesworth - JOY Unspeakable and Full of Glory

shall be saved." [Ac 2.21] Seek him now, call on his name right now; and there is forgiveness, healing, redemption, deliverance, and everything you need for you right here and now, and that which will satisfy you throughout eternity.

"Repeat in your heart often **"baptized with the Holy Ghost and fire, fire, fire!"** All the unction, and weeping, and travailing comes through the baptism of fire, and I say to you and say to myself, purged and cleansed and filled with renewed spiritual power." "Who maketh his ministers a flame of fire." Heb. 1:7

"God wants to purify our minds until we can bear all things, believe all things, hope all things, and endure all things. God dwells in you, but you cannot have this divine power until you live and walk in the Holy Ghost, until the power of the new life is greater than the old life."

"We are not sufficient to think anything as of ourselves, but our sufficiency is of **God**." If you go back, you miss the plan. We leave the old order of things. We can never have confidence in the flesh; we cannot touch that. We are in a new order, a spiritual order. It is a new life of absolute faith in the sufficiency of our **God** in everything that pertains to life and godliness.

*"**There are times when there seems to be a stone wall in front of us. There are times when there are no feelings. There are times when everything seems as black as midnight, and there is nothing left but confidence in God. What you must do is have the devotion and confidence to believe that He will not fail, and cannot fail.**

You will never get anywhere if you depend on your feelings. There is something a thousand times better than feelings, and it is the powerful Word of God. There is a divine revelation within you that came when you were born from above, and this is real faith. To be born into the new KINGDOM is to be born into a new faith."

"Done away! Done away!" Henceforth there is a new cry in our hearts, "I delight to do Thy will, O **God**." He taketh away the first, the ministration of death, written and engrave in stones, that He might establish the second, this ministration of righteousness, this life in the **Spirit**.

How does this new life work out? The thing works out because God works in you to will and to do of His own good pleasure. (Phil. 2:13).

"God has privileged us in Christ Jesus to live above the ordinary human plane of life. Those who want to be ordinary and live on a lower plane can do so, but as for me, I will not."

"Right now, the precious blood of **Jesus Christ** is efficacious to cleanse your heart & bring this **Wonderful** life of **God** in you."

"Is salvation and healing for all? It is for all who will press in and get their portion. The word can drive every disease away from your body. It is your portion in Christ, Him who is our bread, our life, our health, our all in all."

"The power of **God** is beyond all our conception. The trouble is that we do not have the power of **God** in a full manifestation because of our finite thoughts, but as we go on and let **God** have His way, there is no limit to what our limitless **God** will do in response to a limitless faith. But you will never get anywhere except you are in constant pursuit of all the life of **God**."

"God has something better for you than you have ever had in the past. Come out into all the fullness of faith and power and life and victory that He is willing to provide, as you forget the things of the past, and press right on for the prize of His calling in Christ Jesus."

"**God** wants your life to manifest His glory!"

"No-one can live after seeing God; and God wants us ALL to see Him so that we shall joyfully cease to be--and that HE may become our life."

"If you want to increase in the life of **God**, then you must settle it in your heart that you will not at any time resist the **Holy Spirit**. The **Holy Ghost** and fire - the fire burning up everything that would impoverish and destroy you."

"God wants to purify our minds until we can bear all things, believe all things, hope all things, and endure all things. God dwells in you, but you cannot have this divine power until you live and walk in the Holy Ghost, until the power of the new life is greater than the old life."

"Divine life is full of divine appointment and equipping, and you cannot be filled with the power of **God** without a manifestation. It is my prayer that we would understand that to be filled with the **Holy Spirit** is to be filled with manifestation, the glory of the **Lord** being in the midst of us, manifesting His divine power."

"Never look back if you want the power of God in your life. You will find out that in the measure you have allowed yourself to look back, you have missed what God had for you."

"How great is the position of the man who is born of **God**, born of purity, born of faith, born of life, born of power!"

"If you think the life and the power of God comes from you, you are making a great mistake."

"Enter into the promises of **God**. It is your inheritance. You will do more in one year if you are really filled with the Life of the **Holy Ghost** than you could do in fifty years apart from Him."

Smith - "When the saint ceases to seek after holiness, purity, righteousness, truth; when he ceases to pray, stops reading the Word and gives way to carnal appetites, then it is that Satan comes."

Smith Wigglesworth - JOY Unspeakable and Full of Glory

I was once traveling from Belgium to England. As I landed I received a request to stop at a place between Harwich and Colchester. The people were delighted that **God** had sent me, and told me of a special situation that they wanted me to pray for. They said, "We have a brother here who believes in the **Lord**, and he is paralyzed from his loins downward. He cannot stand on his legs and he has been twenty years in this condition." They took me to this man and as I saw him there in his chair I put the question to him. "What is the greatest desire in your heart?"

He said, "Oh, if I could only receive the **Holy Ghost**!" I was somewhat surprised at this answer, and I laid my hands on his head and said, "Receive ye the **Holy Ghost**." Instantly the power of **God** fell upon him and he began breathing very heavily. He rolled off the chair and there he lay like a bag of potatoes, utterly helpless. I love it when **God** is at moving. I like to watch **God** working. There he was with his great, fat body, and his head was swinging just as though it was on a swivel. Then to our **JOY** he began speaking in a heavenly tongue. I had my eyes glued on him and as I saw the condition of his legs I said, "Those legs can never carry that body."

Then I looked up and said, "**Lord**, tell me what to do. "The **Holy Ghost** is the executive of **Jesus Christ** and the Father. If you want to know the mind of **God** you must have the **Holy Ghost** to bring **God**'s latest thought to you and to tell you what to do. The **Lord** said to me, "Command him in My name to walk" But I missed it.

I said to the people there, "Let's see if we can lift him up." But we could not lift him, he was like a ton weight. I cried, "Oh **Lord**, forgive me." I repented of doing the wrong thing, and then the **Lord** said to me again, "Command him to walk." I said to him, "Arise in the name of **Jesus**." His legs were immediately strengthened. Did he walk? YES! He ran all around. A month after this he walked ten miles and back. He has a Pentecostal work now. When the power of the **Holy Ghost** is present, things will happen.

Smith - I am not moved by what I see or feel - but by what I believe!

Sermon: Dare to believe and to command

A needy man came to me in a meeting. He was withered and wasted, in a hopeless condition; death lay in his eyes. He was so helpless he had to have someone on each side to carry him along. He said to me in a whisper, "Can you help me?"

This afflicted man, standing before me so helpless, so withered, he had had cancer of the stomach. The physicians had taken away the cancer from his stomach, but in removing it they had taken away the man's ability to swallow. The cancer was removed, and seemingly his life was spared, but he could not swallow any longer. In order to keep him from starving, they had made an opening in his stomach and inserted a tube about nine inches long, with a cup at the top, and he fed himself with liquids.

Smith Wigglesworth - JOY Unspeakable and Full of Glory

For three months he had managed to keep alive, walking about like a skeleton. Here he was asking whether I could help him. What should I say? I remembered the promise, "If thou canst believe, all things are possible to him that believeth." And again, "He that believeth on me, the works that I do shall he do also; and greater works than these shall he do; because I go unto my Father."

The Word must be true. **Jesus** is with the Father, and therefore even greater works than His can be done if we believe. So I believed, and therefore I spoke.

"Go home and have a good supper," I said. The poor fellow replied, "I cannot swallow." I repeated, "On the authority of the Word of **God** I say it. It is the promise of **Jesus**. Go home in the name of **Jesus**, and have a good supper." He went home. Supper was prepared. Many times before this he had taken food in his mouth and had been forced to spit it out again. But I had believed **God**. (I am here to inspire you.) I am a natural man, just as you are, but I dared to believe that he would swallow that night.

So after he had filled his mouth with food, he chewed it, and then it went right down his throat. He ate until he was quite satisfied. He and his family went to bed filled with **JOY**. The next morning when they arose they were filled with the same **JOY**. Life had begun again, it seemed. The man looked down to see the opening which the physicians had made into his stomach, but it was gone. He did not need two openings, so when **God** opened the natural passage He closed the other.

That is what **God** is like all the time. He brings things to pass when we believe and trust him. **God** wants you to realize this truth. Dare to believe, then dare to speak, and you shall have whatsoever you say.

Faith in the living word

Every day I live I am more and more convinced that very few who are saved by the grace of **God** have the divine revelation of how great is their authority over darkness, demons, death and every power of the enemy by the name of **Jesus Christ**. It is a real **JOY** when we realize our inheritance on this line.

I was speaking like this one day, and someone said, "I have never heard anything like this before. How many months did it take you to put together this sermon?" I said, "Brother, **God** impress upon my wife from time to time to get me to preach, and I promised her I would. I used to labor hard for a week to get a message together. I would simply give out my text and then sit down and say, 'I am done.' O brother, I have given up getting the messages together anymore.

They all come down from heaven, and the sermons that come down as He wants them. Then they go back to **God**, with much results in fruit, for the Word of **God** declares that His Word shall not return unto Him void. If you get anything from **God**, it will be fresh from heaven. But these messages were also transform you as you speak them.

Smith Wigglesworth - JOY Unspeakable and Full of Glory

Smith - It is God's delight to make possible to us that which seems impossible.

I want all you people to totally delivered, all to be filled with peace, all to be without pain or sickness, I want all to be free. There is a man here with great pain in his head, I am going to lay my hands on him in the name of **Jesus** and he shall tell you what **God** has done.

I believe that would be the right thing to do, before I begin to preach to you, to help this poor man so that he shall enjoy the meeting like us, without any pain. (The man referred to was in pain with his head wrapped up in a bandage), and after he was prayed for he testified that he had absolutely no pain.

His LOVE in You & in Me

I want you to notice that I am trying to show you, by the grace of **God**, that if you keep in the fullness of the **Spirit** you will have such a revelation of the Word of **God** in your life that it will save you and keep you from stumbling.

"The angel of the **Lord** encampeth round about them that fear Him and delivereth him." And, "The steps of a good man are ordered of the **Lord**." He shall hide thee in the secret place, in the cleft of the rock, and in the time of adversity He shall raise up a standard against the enemy.

It is the **Lord** who reigns supreme over His household whose House ye are, His establishment, and ye shall not be moved. This means that **God** establishes His KINGDOM in you and in me. Oh how we need to be filled with the **JOY** of the **Lord** which is our strength and to have a fresh inflow of His life and love!

A man who is filled with the **Spirit** must have three things flowing through him; the ministration, operation and manifestation of the **Spirit**. It is to your detriment if you have not these three working in your life.

If you are to keep your path all clear and bright you must remain steadfast, unmovable, always abounding in the work of the **Lord**. We must abound in hope, **Rejoice** in tribulation and then **God** will make straight paths for our feet.

The man who has faith is never ruffled; he does not run off as if he had been shot but he is always resting, knowing that **God** is over all. We must understand these principles because faith is **God**. Faith is the knowledge of **God**. Faith is that which lays hold, which will not let go. Faith is inwrought **God**, faith is **God** inwrought; faith is that which brings heaven on earth and lives in it.

Multitudes of sinners healed

Multitudes of awful sinners were healed. A whole family (all wicked) was saved through being healed. **Jesus** is glorious. Surely He is the most lovely of all. Truly He was manifested to destroy the works of the devil. That Name manifests life as truly as ever it did.

Life in the Spirit

(Wigglesworth) I don't want to boast. If I glory in anything, it is only in the **Lord** who has been so gracious to me. But I remember one time stepping out of a railroad carriage to wash my hands. I had a season of prayer, and the **Lord** just filled me to overflowing with His love. I was going to a convention in Ireland, and I could not get there fast enough.

As I returned, I believe that the **Spirit** of the **Lord** was so heavily upon me that my face must have shone. (No man can tell himself when the **Spirit** transforms his very countenance.) There were two clerical mere sitting together, and as I got into the carriage again, one of them cried out, "You convince me of sin." Within three minutes every one in the carriage was crying to **God** for salvation.

This thing has happened many times in my life. It is this ministration of the **Spirit** that Paul speaks of, this filling of the **Spirit**, that will make your life effective, so that even the people in the stores where you trade will want to leave your presence because they are brought under conviction.

"Beloved, now are we the sons of **God**, and it doth not yet appear what we shall be; but we know that when He shall appear we shall be like Him for we shall see Him as He is; and everyone that hath this hope purifieth himself even as He is pure." It is the hope of the Church, the Bridegroom coming for the bride. He has suffered for us, been buried for us, risen for us, is jealous for us. How we should love Him! He is coming again and He wants us to be ready.

JESUS REVEALED

Wherever **Jesus** came sin was revealed and men don't like sin revealed. Sin, separates from **God** for ever. You are in a good place when you weep before **God**, repenting over the least thing. If you have spoken unkindly, you realize it was not like the **Lord**. Your keen conscience has taken you to prayer. It is a **Wonderful** thing to have a keen conscience. It is when we are close to **God** that our hearts are revealed. **God** intends us to live in purity— seeing Him all the time.

When I am leaving anywhere by train or ship, people come to see me off, and I preach to them. The Captain hears, the stewards hear. "Oh," they said, "another on board!" The world thinks there is something wrong with you if you are full of zeal for **God**.

A young man came and asked me to take part in a sweepstake. I said, "I am preaching on Sunday—would you come if I did?" He said, "No." Later, there was an entertainment. I said I would take a part. It was the strangest thing for me. I said I would sing. I saw men dressed as clergy entertaining the people with foolishness. I was troubled. I cried to **God**.

Then came my turn just before the dance. A young woman came to take my book—she was half dressed. She said, "I cannot play that." I said, "Never worry." I sang, "Oh, if I could only tell you how I love Him, I am sure that you would make Him yours today." There was no dance! They began weeping, and six young men gave their hearts to **God** in my cabin.

The world does not know us, but we are sons of **God** with power. No man that sins has power. Sin makes a man weak. Remember this—sin dethrones, but purity strengthens. Temptation is not sin; but the devil is a liar and tries to take away our peace. You must live in the Word of **God**. There is now no condemnation.

Who is he that can condemn you? **Christ** has died. He won't condemn you. He died to save you. Don't condemn yourself. If there is anything wrong, come to the Blood. "If we walk in the light as He is in the Light, we have fellowship one with another, and the blood of **Jesus**, **God**'s Son, cleanseth us from all sin."

Jesus was manifested to destroy the works of the devil. You can come into a new experience of **God** where **God** creates in our hearts such a love for **Jesus** that we are living in a new realm— Sons of **God** with power, filled with all the fullness of **God**.

Smith Wigglesworth - JOY Unspeakable and Full of Glory

"Whom having not seen, ye love."

Oh, how sweet! There is no voice so gentle, so soft, so full of tenderness to me, as His; and no touch. Is it possible to love Him when we have not seen Him? **God** will make it possible; and, "though now ye see him not, yet believing," He will enable you to "**Rejoice** with **JOY** unspeakable and full of glory," **Rejoice**! We have something to **Rejoice** over. Oh, what a salvation **God** has provided for us in all our worthlessness and nothingness and helplessness!

I entreat you from the **Lord** to be so reconciled to Him that there will be no division between you and Him. Will you give Him preeminence in all things? Shall He not have His rightful place, and decide for you the way and plan of your life?

Beloved, when you allow Him to decide for you, when you want nothing but His blessed will, when He is in very deed **Lord** and Sovereign of all, you will have a foretaste of heaven all the time. The **Lord** bless you with grace to leave all and say, "I will follow Thee, **Lord Jesus**."

Smith - "The moment a man falls into sin, divine life ceases to flow, and his life becomes one of helplessness."

Sermon: On resurrection power

Last week I went into a house where they were very much in great distress. A young woman was there who, they told me, had not been able to drink for six years. Her body had been rapidly degrading, but the **Lord** had inspired her with faith and she said to her father, "O Father, I ought to have relief to-day. Somehow I feel this whole trouble ought to go to-day." I knew what it was. It was a demon in the throat. I believe that the devil is at the bottom of practically every evil in human lives. It was a serious thing to see that beautiful young woman, who, because of this one thing in her life, was so disorganized in her mind and body. I knew it was the power of Satan. How did I know? Because it attacked her at a vital point, and the thing had preyed on her mind and she was filled with fear so that she said, "I dare not drink, for if I do I shall choke."

Deliverance to the captives. I asked the father and mother to go out of the room and then I said to the young woman, "You will be free and drink as much as you want when I have done with you if you will only believe. As sure as you are there you will drink as much as you want." I said further, "Our brethren are going out in the streets to preach to-night and I shall be among them, and in our preaching we will say definitely, 'Every one that will believe on the **Lord Jesus Christ** can be saved.' We will also tell them that everyone that believes can be healed.

The Word of **God** shows us plainly that the Son of **God** bore our sins and our sicknesses at Calvary. They will emphasize it over and over again. It is just as true to say, 'Himself took our infirmities and bare our sicknesses,' as it is to say, 'He was wounded for our transgressions, He was bruised for our iniquities.' " So I said to her, "Now do you believe?" She said, "Yes, I believe that in the name of **Jesus** you can cast the evil power out." I then laid my hands on her in the name of **Jesus**. "It is done, you drink."

She went out laughingly and drew the first glass of water and drank. She cried out, "Mother! Father! Brother! I have drunk one glass!" There was **JOY** in the house. What did it? It was the living faith of the Son of **God**. Oh, if we only knew how rich we are, and how near we are to the Fountain of life. "All things are possible to him that believeth."

A PLACE OF ZEAL, POWER, PASSION

When we came into this new work **God** spoke to us by the **Spirit** and we knew we had to reach the place of absolute submission and cleansing, so that there would be nothing left. We were swept and garnished.

Now, that was only the beginning, and if you have not made spiritual progress into that **Holy** place of zeal, power and COMPASSION for **God**, we can truly say you have backslidden in heart. The backslider in heart is dead to Gods fullness. He is not having the open vision. The backslider in heart is not seeing the Word of **God** living and fresh every day.

You can put it down that a man is a backslider in heart if does not hate the sinful things of the world. And if you have the applause of the world you do not having the approval of **God**.

I do not know whether you will receive it or not but my heart burns with this message, "changing in the regeneration" for in this changing you will get a place in the kingdom to come where you shall be in authority; that place which **God** has prepared for us, that place which is beyond all human conception.

We can catch a glimpse of that glory, when we see how John worshipped the angel, and the angel said to him, **"See thou do it not, for I am thy fellow-servant, of thy brethren the prophets."** This angel is showing John the wonders of the glorious kingdom and in his glorified state, John thought he was the **Lord**. I wonder if we dare believe for this glorious place.

"lamb without blemish and without spot"

When John saw Him, the Revelation that he had was that He was the **"lamb without blemish and without spot" (1 Pet. 1:19)**. When revelation comes, it says, **"In Him dwells all the fullness" (Col. 2:9)**.

His character is beautiful. His display of meekness is lovely. His COMPASSION is greater than that of anyone in all of humanity. He felt our infirmities. He helps those who are going through trials. And it is to be said about Him what is not said about anyone else: **"[He] was in all points tempted as we are, yet without sin" (Heb. 4:15)**.

I want you, as the author of Hebrews wonderfully said, to **"consider Him who endured such hostility from sinners against Himself, lest you become weary and discouraged in your souls" (Heb. 12:3)**. When you are weary, tempted, tried and

Smith Wigglesworth - JOY Unspeakable and Full of Glory

all men are against you, consider Him who has passed through it all, so that He might be able to help you in the trial as you are passing through it.

He will sustain you in the struggle. When all things seem to indicate that you have failed, the **Lord** of Hosts, the **God** of Jacob, the one who is salvation, our **Christ** will so establish you that you will be stronger than any concrete building that was ever constructed by man.

Paul was an example for the church. He was filled with the loveliness of the character of the Master through the **Spirit**'s power. He was zealous that we may walk worthy of the **Lord**. This is the day of calling that he spoke about; this is the opportunity of our lifetime. This is the place where **God** increases strength and opens doors for a new way of ministry.

Thought for today: If there is anything in your life that in any way resists the power of the Holy Spirit and the entrance of His Word into your heart and life, drop on your knees and cry aloud for mercy. That you may be able to be changed from glory to glory.

Smith - It is impossible to overestimate the importance of being filled with the Spirit

At one time there was brought to me a beautiful young woman who had been fascinated with some preacher, and just because he had not taken interest in her on the line of courtship and marriage, the devil took advantage and made her fanatical and mad. They brought her 250 miles in that condition. She had previously received the Baptism in the **Spirit**. You ask, "can a demon come in to a person that has been baptized in the

Holy Ghost?" Our only place of safety is if we are going on with **God** and in constantly being filled with the **Holy Ghost**.

You must not forget Demas. He must have been baptized with the **Holy Ghost** for he appears to have been a right-hand worker with Paul, but the enemy got him to the place where he loved this present world and he dropped off. When they brought this young woman to me the evil power was immediately discerned and immediately I cast this demonic thing out in the name of **Jesus**. It was a great **JOY** to present her before all the people in her right mind again. The devil has no power against the name of **Jesus**.

Smith - None of you can be strong in God unless you are diligently & constantly listening to what He has to say through His Word.

After receiving the Baptism in the **Holy Ghost** and speaking in tongues as the **Spirit** gave utterance, I did not speak with tongues again for nine months. I was troubled about it because I went up and down laying hands upon people that they might receive the **Holy Ghost**, and they were speaking in tongues, but I did not have the **JOY** of speaking in tongues myself.

God wanted to show me that the speaking in tongues as the **Spirit** gave utterance, which I received when I received the Baptism, was distinct from the gift of tongues which I received at a later date. When I laid hands on other people and they received the **Holy Ghost**,

Smith Wigglesworth - JOY Unspeakable and Full of Glory

I used to think, "Oh, **Lord Jesus**, it would be nice if You would let me speak." He withheld the gift from me, for He knew that I would meet many who would say that the Baptism of the **Holy Ghost** can be received without the speaking in tongues, and that people simply received the gift of tongues when they received the Baptism.

I did not receive the gift of tongues at that time, but nine months later I was going out of the door one morning, speaking to the **Lord** in my own heart, when there came out of my mouth a new tongue. When the tongues stopped I said to the **Lord**, "Now, **Lord**, I did not do it, and I wasn't seeking it; so You have done it, and I am not going to move from this place until you give me the interpretation."

And then came an interpretation which has been fulfilled all the world over. Is it the **Holy Ghost** who speaks? Then the **Holy Ghost** can interpret. Let him that speaks in a unknown tongue pray that he may interpret, and **God** will give the interpretation. We must not rush through without getting a clear understanding of what **God** has to say to us by his supernatural gifts, which are given by the **Holy Ghost**.

CHAPTER SEVEN

Smith - When we get to the place where we take no thought of ourselves, then God takes thought for us.

On Monday, after Matthew was healed, Mr. Wigglesworth started up the road with a brother, when the **Lord** said to him, "That woman with the apron on up the road is not saved." He mentioned to the brother the impression he had and when he neared the woman he said, "The **Lord** convinced me coming up the road that you do not know Him and that you want to be saved." Instantly she spoke out loudly that for three weeks she had been under conviction and wanted salvation. They went into the cottage across the way and **God** instantly saved her.

Going from there to Grantham to take the train he

Smith Wigglesworth - JOY Unspeakable and Full of Glory

stopped to see the mother of a young woman who had been converted in their mission in Bradford. When he reached her house she said, "Don't stop here. Go with that man on his bicycle," pointing to a man some distance off. Before they reached the house they heard a voice crying out, "Oh, dear me!" "Oh, dear me!" When they got inside they found a man suffering terrible agony and distress.

At first Brother Wigglesworth thought he was sent there that the man might be healed, but instead of that he asked, "Are you saved?" The sick man cried out, "I would give the world! I would die comfortable if I were." Brother Wigglesworth pointed him to the Way of salvation, rebuked the unbelief, and instantly the man realized that he had passed from death into life and the shout of **JOY** took the place of the cry of distress. His wife, seeing the **JOY** that came to her husband, fell down at his bedside and cried for salvation. He was not led to pray for the sick man's healing and in three hours he went sweeping through the gates of heaven.

(12) QUOTES ON: ETERNAL LIFE

SMITH WIGGLESWORTH

The soul, covered with the blood, has moved from a natural to an eternal union with the **Lord**. Instead of death will be the fullness of life divine."

"We have a big God. We have a Wonderful Jesus. We have a glorious Comforter. God's canopy is over you and will cover you at all times, preserving you from evil. Under His wings shalt thou trust. The Word of God is living and powerful and in its treasures you will find eternal life. If you dare trust this Wonderful Lord, the Lord of life, you will find in Him everything you need."

"These words were among the greatest that **Jesus** ever spoke: "The hour has come." Time was finished and eternity has begun for every soul that is covered with the blood. Until that hour, all people lived only to die, but the moment the sacrifice was made, it was not the end but only the beginning. The soul, covered with the blood, has moved from a natural to an eternal union with the **Lord**. Instead of death will be the fullness of life divine."

It is not only to be saved, my brother, but that there is an eternal destiny awaiting us of wonderment that God has for us in the glory.

We are called to be eternally saved by the power of **God**. Do not be led astray by anything, do not go by your feelings for your salvation, and do not take anybody's word for your salvation. Believe that **God**'s Word is true. What does it say?

"He that hath the Son hath life; he that hath not the Son shall not see life, but the wrath of God abideth upon him."

You can receive something in three minutes that you can carry with you into glory. What do you want? Is anything too hard for God? God can meet you now. God sees inwardly, He knows all about you. Nothing is hidden from Him, and He can satisfy the soul and give you a spring of eternal blessing that will carry you right through.

Smith Wigglesworth - JOY Unspeakable and Full of Glory

We are **God**'s own children, quickened by his **Spirit** and he has given us power over all the powers of darkness; **Christ** in us the open evidence of eternal glory, **Christ** in us the life, the truth and the way.

The natural man cannot receive it, but the spiritual man, the man who has been created anew by faith in **Christ**, he is able to receive it. The man who believes **God** comes in into our hearts with the eternal seed of truth and righteousness and faith, and from the moment he sees the truth by faith he is made a new creation.

Oh, the remarkableness of our Lord Jesus! I want to impress upon you the importance of realizing that Jesus is in the midst. No person need be without the knowledge that they are not only saved, but that God can live in their bodies.

You are begotten the moment you believe, unto a lively hope. "He that believeth hath eternal life." [Jn 3.36] You have eternal life the moment you believe. The first life is temporal, natural, material, but in the new birth you exist as long as God Himself! Forever!

And we are begotten by an incorruptible power, by the word of God. The new birth is unto righteousness, begotten by God the moment that you believe. God always saves through the heart. He that believeth in his heart and confesseth with his mouth shall be saved. [Ro 10.9]

We are born of the incorruptible Word of **God** which liveth and abideth for ever, which made the world and brought into existence things that were not there, and there was nothing made but what He made, and so I realize I am made twice.

I was made first by the creation of **God**. The next time I was begotten in a moment of time, eternally begotten, and if you believe in your heart you can begin to say, and whatsoever you say will come to pass if you believe in your heart.

Live in the Spirit till sin has no dominion. "That as sin hath reigned unto death, even so might grace reign through righteousness unto eternal life by Jesus Christ our Lord." (Rom. 5.) Reigning in life.

AMAZING NEW LIFE

One day Smith and his wife received a letter from a young man asking for prayer. He had been healed about three years before of a bad foot, and they had lost all trace of him since, until this urgent cry came from a home where in the natural, death was soon to enter. When the letter came Mrs. Wigglesworth said to her husband, "If you go, **God** will give you this case." He telegraphed back that he would go.

Wigglesworth got on his bicycle riding from Grantham, nine miles away to Willsford. When he reached the village he inquired where the young man, Matthew Snell, lived. This young man had heart failure and had to lie perfectly still in one place. The doctor said if he moved from that place he would surely die, and left him, never expecting to see him alive again. When Mr. Wigglesworth reached the house, the mother of the young man stood in the doorway and said, "Oh you have come too late." "Is he alive at all?" He asked the mother. "Yes, he is just barely alive."

Smith went into the parlor where he was lying. The young man, Matthew, said in a barely audible voice, "I cannot rise, I am too weak, and the doctor says if I turn around I shall die." Mr. Wigglesworth said this to him, "Matthew, the **Lord** is the strength of your heart and thy portion altogether. Will you believe that the **Lord** will raise you up for His glory?"

Smith Wigglesworth - JOY Unspeakable and Full of Glory

The young man answered, "**Lord**, if You will raise me up for Your glory I will give You my life." Hands were laid on him in the name of the **Lord Jesus Christ** and instantly new life came into him. "Shall I arise?" he asked, but Wigglesworth felt in his heart that the young man should lie perfectly quiet and so advised. The night was spent in prayer and the next morning Brother Wigglesworth attended the ten o'clock meeting in the Primitive Methodist Chapel. He was asked to speak and talked of faith in **God**, and from that moment the unbelief seemed to clear away from the village people.

They came to him at the close of the service and said, "We believe Matthew will be raised up." He had asked the family to air Matthew's clothing for him for that he could wear them, but they did not do it because they did not believe he would be healed.

For six weeks he had been in a very serious condition, becoming weaker all the time. Mr. Wigglesworth strongly insisted on them preparing Matthew's clothes. They finally relented not because they believed for healing, but to satisfy him. About 2:30 he went into the room where the young man lay and said,

"Now I would like this to be for the glory of **God**. It shall never be said that Wigglesworth raised you up." The young man answered, "For Thy glory, **Lord**; my life shall be for Thee." Then the servant of the **Lord** said, "Matthew, I believe the moment I lay hands on you the glory of **God** will fill this place so I shall not be able to stand."

As he did this the glory of the **Lord** fell upon them until he fell on his face to the floor; it increased until everything in the room shook, the bed and Matthew who was on the bed, and with a strong voice the young man cried out, "For Thy glory, **Lord** !" "For Thy glory!"

This continued for at least fifteen minutes, when it was apparent to them **God** would give him strength not only to rise but to dress

125

in the glorious power which seemed like the description given of the temple being filled with the glory of **God**, and the young man was walking up and down, shouting and praising **God** and clapping his hands.

He went to the door and called to his father that the **Lord** had raised him up. His father was a backslider and fell down before **God** and cried for mercy. His sister, who had been brought out of an asylum and was threatened with another attack of insanity, in the manifestation of that glory was delivered from that time. That weak body immediately became strong, eating regular food immediately.

The doctor came and examined his heart and declared it was all right. Matthew declared it should be for the **Lord**'s glory and at once began preaching in the power of the **Holy Ghost**. His own statement is that when he gives the story of his healing many are saved.

Smith - See to it there is never anything comes out of your lips or by your acts that will interfere with the work of the Lord

A young woman came into Smith's mission one night and was so impressed with what she heard that at the close she said to Mrs. Wigglesworth: "There is a young woman at Allerton who has been living there for six years and never been outside the door. Will you go up there?" Mrs. Wigglesworth referred her to her husband and he said he would go. As he started down the road, which was filled with people traveling to and fro, the **Holy Ghost** fell upon him so that he stood in the street and shouted for **JOY**, and the tears rained down his face and saturated his waistcoat.

Smith Wigglesworth - JOY Unspeakable and Full of Glory

To his astonishment, nobody in the street seemed to recognize his condition; it seemed as though the **Lord** covered him. He dared not speak to anybody lest the presence of the **Lord** should leave him. The young woman who went with him was full of talk, but he said nothing. As soon as he entered the house the glory of **God** came more fully upon him and as he lay hands on this poor afflicted woman the glory of **God** filled the house. He was so filled with **God**'s glory he rushed out of the house and the young woman running after him exclaiming, "How did you get this glory? Tell me! Tell me!" He told her to go back into the house and seek the **Lord**.

A week after that he was in an office in Bradford and as soon as he entered the office a man said, "Wigglesworth, sit down. I want to tell you something." He sat down to listen, and the office-man said, "Last Sunday night at the chapel the preacher was in the midst of preaching when suddenly the door swung open, and in came a young woman who had been confined to her home for six years.

She stood up and said that as she came out of the house the heavens were covered with the most glorious light and presence of **God**, and she read over the heavens. 'The **Lord** is coming soon.'" Mr. Wigglesworth wept and praised **God**, but said nothing. He realized that **God** wanted him to know the young lady had been healed but that he was not to talk about it.

Smith - Now hear this. Faith knows no defeat!

At Victoria Halt there came a woman pressed down with cancer of the breast. She was anointed with oil, according to **God**'s Word. I laid hands on the cancer, cast out the demon, immediately the cancer which had up to then been bleeding, dried up. She received a deep impression through the **Spirit** that the work was done, and closely watched the healing process together with a lady friend.

The cancer began to move from its seat, and in five days dropped out entirely into the protecting bandage. They were greatly blessed and full of **JOY**, and when looking into the cavity from whence the tumor had come, they saw to their amazement and surprise that not one drop of blood had been shed at the separation of the cancer. The cavity was sufficiently large to receive a small cup and they noticed that the sides were of a beautiful reddish hue.

During the next two days, and while they were watching closely they saw the cavity fill up with flesh and a skin formed over it, so that at last there was only a slight scar. At two meetings this lady, filled with enthusiasm, held in her hand a glass vessel containing the cancer, and declared how great things **God** had done unto her.

Smith Wigglesworth - JOY Unspeakable and Full of Glory

Smith - Some people would be giants in faith if only they had a shout!

Here was another woman unable to walk, sitting on a chair as she was ministered to. Her experience was the same as hundreds of the others. She rose up, looking around, wondering if after all it was a dream. Suddenly she laughed and said, "My leg is healed." Afterwards she said, "I am not saved," and streams of tears ran down her face. They prayed for her, and later she left the meeting healed and saved and full of **JOY**. We have a **Wonderful** Savior; glory to His **Holy** Name!

Smith - They think I am rather unmerciful in my dealing with the sick. No, I have no mercy for the devil.

Published in Melbourne Argos

Further demonstrations of "healing by touch" were given by Mr. Smith Wigglesworth, a Yorkshire evangelist, before a very large assemblage at the Olympia last night. After the evangelist had given an address on the subject of "Faith," he called upon those who had come "for aid" on Tuesday night to testify as to the results; and several persons who had been suffering front deafness, rheumatics, and lameness declared that their ailments had completely gone.

Mr. Wigglesworth healing by touch." An elderly man, who said that he had been deaf for years, cried **"Hallellujah! Hallellujah!"** when asked by Mr.

Wigglesworth if he could hear, after hands had been placed on him and he had been prayed over. A woman who, who had stiff legs for over 20 years, and who limped to Olympia on the arm of a relative, ran about the hall in **JOY** after she had been "touched." Another woman, who was said to have been an invalid in a chair for 23 years, declared that her limbs were "beginning to move." She was advised by the evangelist to retain her faith in **Jesus Christ** and her cure; would be complete.

A young woman with pains of long standing "in her back was able to stoop and touch the ground with her hands, and she laughed heartily as she told the audience that her trouble had gone. A woman, who asserted that she had been unable to walk owing to pain in her feet, ran up and down in front of the audience, crying, "Praise the name of the **Lord**." She declared that her pain vanished when the evangelist touched her.

Smith - God works mightily when you persist in believing Him.

I feel I must express my deep gratitude for blessing received. Only those who have been in the furnace of affliction can realize the **JOY** of deliverance. It seems too **Wonderful**. After fourteen years of anguish, sleeplessness, and spiritual depression, caused by the bondage of the adversary, these are things of the past.

As Bro. Wigglesworth says, consumption is of the devil, and only the Lion of Judah could have delivered

Smith Wigglesworth - JOY Unspeakable and Full of Glory

me from this dread scourge, which had made my body a mass of corruption. **Hallellujah!** KATHLEEN GAY.

Smith - Remember, the most trying time is the most helpful time. In your weakness, God will make you strong.

The follow-on meetings have been wonderfully blessed. One woman in the Sunday morning meeting, after Brother Wigglesworth had left, was healed of three diseases. She came on the following Wednesday bringing fifteen friends with her, eleven of whom were saved that night as we gave the altar call.

I had the job of immersing eight in water while Brother Wigglesworth was here. The youngest being a Singhalese girl, seven years old. She had a **Wonderful** testimony, and on the morning of her baptism, she had a vision of **Jesus**. It was a **JOY** to my soul to take her in my arms and bury her with **Christ** in the water.

Smith – Never trust human plans. God will work mightily when you persist in believing His plan.

The hall held 1,800 people. At nearly every meeting crowds were unable to enter the building, but they waited on often hours and hours for the chance, if any left the building, to step into the place. Here a man with two crutches, his whole body shaking with palsy, is lifted on to the platform. (Behind him five or six hundred more are waiting for help.)

This man is anointed and hands laid upon him in the Name of **Jesus**. He is still shaking. Then he drops one crutch, and after a short time the other one. His body is still shaking, but he takes the first step out in faith! Will it be? He lifts one foot and then the other, walks round the platform. The onlookers **Rejoice** with him. Now he walks around the auditorium. **Hallellujah!**

Smith – When you take up God's Word, you get the truth. Remember, God is not a man that He should lie.

"It will **Rejoice** your heart to hear the beautiful testimonies which are still coming in from those who were helped and blest in your meetings here in Australia. The dear people do not forget those beautiful spiritual feasts they had every morning. Do you remember that dear woman in J,---- who was too ill to be brought in the church?

She was put in the vestry, had to be carried in, was wrapped up in bandages. Well, she is now a living miracle, is going around doing her own work as well as anyone. It was a Baptist minister who brought this woman and he is now seeking to be filled with the **Holy Ghost**.

WONDERFUL SALVATION

Smith - "I know that God's word is sufficient. One word from Him can change a nation. His word is from everlasting to everlasting. It is through the entrance of this everlasting Word, this incorruptible seed, that we are born again, and come into this Wonderful salvation. Man cannot live by bread alone, but must live by every word that proceeded out of the mouth of God. This is the food of faith. "Faith cometh by hearing, and hearing by the Word of God."

In a place in England I was teaching on the lines of faith and what would take place if we believed **God**. Many **Wonderful** things were happening. When I was done teaching it appeared one man who worked in a coal mine had heard me. He was in trouble with a very stiff knee. He said to his wife, "I cannot help but think every day that that message of Wigglesworth's was to stir us to do something. I cannot get it out of my mind. All the men in the pit know how I walk with a stiff knee, and you know how you have wrapped it around with yards of flannel.

Well, I am going to act. You have to be the congregation." He got his wife in front of him. "I am going to act and do just as Wigglesworth did." He got hold of his leg unmercifully, saying, **"Come out, you devils, come out! In the name of Jesus.** Now, **Jesus, help me. Come out, you devils, come out."** Then he said, "Wife they are gone! Wife, they are gone. This is too good. I am going to act now." So he went to his place of worship and all the other coal workers were there. It was a prayer meeting.

As he told them this story these men became delighted. They said, "Jack, come over here and help me." And Jack went. As soon as he was through in one home he was invited to another, delivering and losing these people of the pains they had gotten in the coal mine.

Smith - There are 4 principles we need to maintain: 1 READ the Word. 2 CONSUME the Word. 3 BELIEVE the Word. 4 ACT on the Word.

I was asked to visit a man in a mental institution, a slave to alcoholism and nicotine. The evil power would not allow me to approach this man. But **God** gave me **Wonderful** authority over the power of this evil **Spirit** that was at work in him. Immediately **God** granted that a broken and contrite heart was given to him, and he was crying out for salvation. In just three short days he was out of that place. In the Name: of **Jesus** we dealt with the two evil powers—the hardest thing in life was to do without tobacco— but the mighty power of **God** came over him.

Smith Wigglesworth - JOY Unspeakable and Full of Glory

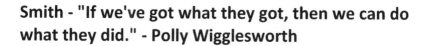

Smith - "If we've got what they got, then we can do what they did." - Polly Wigglesworth

At one meeting there were 1,000 people extremely excited to hear the Word of **God** and about healing. **God** only knows how I have longed to see people saved, and **God** showed me in the **Spirit** He would save. People put up their hands all over the place, as they wanted to be saved. Oh how **Wonderful** it was to see how they flocked to **God**. **God** is the same **God**.

Smith - Every new revelation brings a new dedication.

Sermon: Gifts of Healings, and Miracles

In a meeting a young man stood up, a pitiful object, with a face full of sorrow.

I said, "What is it, young man?" He said he was unable to work, because he could barely walk. He said, "I am so helpless. I have consumption and a weak heart, and my body is full of pain."

I said, "I will pray for you." I said to the people, "As I pray for this young man, I want you to look at his face and see it change."

As I prayed his face changed and there was a **Wonderful** transformation. I said to him, now "Go out and run a mile and come back to the meeting."

He came back and said, "I can now breathe freely."

These meetings continuing but I did not seem any longer. After a few days I saw him again in the meeting. I said, "Young man, tell the people what **God** has done for you."

"Oh," he said, "I have been back to work. I bought some papers to sell and I have made $4.50." Praise **God**, this **Wonderful** stream of salvation never runs dry. You can take a deep drink, it is close to you. It is a river that is running deep and there is plenty for all who are thirsty.

Smith - You will do more in one year if you are really filled with the Holy Ghost than you could do in fifty years apart from Him.

In a meeting a man rose and said, "Will you touch me, I am in a terrible way. I have a family of children, and through an accident in the in the coal mines and I have had no work for two years. I cannot open my hands."

I was full of sorrow for this poor man and something happened which had never come before. We are in the infancy of this **Wonderful** outpouring of the **Holy Spirit** and there is so much more for us. I put out my hand, and before my hands reached his, he was loosed and made perfectly free.

TEACHING FROM SMITH WIGGLESWOTH

Smith Wigglesworth - JOY Unspeakable and Full of Glory

YOU DO NOT NEED drugs, quacks, pills and plasters. We have a big God. We have a Wonderful Jesus. We have a glorious Comforter. God's canopy is over you and will cover you at all times, preserving you from evil. Under His wings shalt thou trust. The Word of God is living and powerful and in its treasures you will find eternal life. If you dare trust this Wonderful Lord, this Lord of life, you will find in Him everything you need.

So many are tampering with drugs, quacks, pills and plasters. Clear them all out and believe God. It is sufficient to believe God. You will find that if you dare trust Him, He will never fail. "The prayer of faith shall save the sick, and the LORD shall raise him up." Do you trust Him? He is worthy to be trusted.

Cry out to God

Are you oppressed? Cry out to **God**. It is always good for people to cry out. You may have to cry out. The **Holy Ghost** and the word of **God** will bring to light every hidden, unclean thing that must be revealed. There is always a place of deliverance when you let **God** search out that which is spoiling and marring your life.

That evil **Spirit** that was in the man in the synagogue cried out, "Let us alone!" [**Lk 4.34**] It was a singular thing that the evil **Spirit** had never cried out like that until **Jesus** walked into the place where he was. **Jesus** rebuked the thing, saying, "Hold thy peace and come out of him," and the man was delivered. [**Lk 4.35**]

He is just the same **Jesus**, exposing the powers of evil, delivering the captives and letting the oppressed go free, purifying them and cleansing their hearts. Those evil spirits that inhabited the man who had the legion did not want to be sent to the pit to be tormented before their time, and so they cried out to be sent into the swine. [**Lk 8.31-32**] Hell is such an awful place that even the demons hate the thought of going there. How much more should men seek to be saved from the pit?

God is COMPASSIONate and says, **"Seek ye the Lord while he may be found." [Is 55.6]** And He has further stated, **"Whosoever shall call on the name of the Lord shall be saved." [Ac 2.21]** Seek him now, call on his name right now; and there is forgiveness, healing, redemption, deliverance, and everything you need for you right here and now, and that which will satisfy you throughout eternity.

I had Great COMPASSION

The Scriptures do not tell false stories. They tell the truth. I want you to know the truth, and the truth will set you free. What is truth? **Jesus** said, **"I am the Way, the Truth, and the Life." "He that believes on Me, as the**

Smith Wigglesworth - JOY Unspeakable and Full of Glory

Scriptures have said, out of his innermost being shall flow forth rivers of living water."

This He spake of the Spirit that should be given them after Jesus was glorified. I do not find anything in the Bible but holiness, and nothing in the world but worldliness. Therefore if I live in the world I shall become worldly; but, on the other hand, if I live in the Bible, I shall become **Holy**.

This is the truth, and the truth will set you free. The power of **God** can we make you. He can actually make you to where you hate sin and love righteousness. He can take away bitterness and hatred and covetousness and malice, and can so consecrate you by His power, through His blood, in nature that you are made pure and every bit **Holy**.

Pure in mind, heart and actions. **God** has given me the way of life, and I want to give it to you, as though this were the last day I had to live. **Jesus** is the best there is for you, and you can each take Him away with you. **God** gave His Son to be the propitiation for your sins, and not only so, but also for the sins of the whole world.

Jesus came to make us free from sin and free from disease and pain. When I see any who are diseased and in pain, I have great COMPASSION for them, and when I lay my hands upon them, I know **God** means men to be so filled with Him that the power of sin shall have no effect upon them, and they shall go forth, as I am doing, to help the needy, sick, and afflicted.

But what is the main thing? To preach the Kingdom of **God** and His righteousness. **Jesus** came to do this. John came preaching repentance. The disciples began by preaching repentance towards **God**, and faith in the **Lord Jesus Christ**, and I tell you, beloved, if you have really been changed by **God**, there is a repentance in your heart never to be repented of.

Through the revelation of the Word of **God** we find that divine healing is solely for the glory of **God**, and salvation is to make you to know that now you have to be inhabited by another, even **God**, and you have.

AMAZING PASSION

A very needy person came to me in a meeting once, all withered and wasted. He had no hope. There was nothing but death in his eyes. He was so helpless that he had to have someone on each side to bear him up. He came to me and said in a whisper, "Can you help me?" Will **Jesus** answer? **"He that believeth on Me, the works that I do shall he do also; and greater works than these…. Behold, I give you power… over all the power of the enemy."**

These are the words of our **Lord Jesus**. It is not our word but the word of the **Lord**, and as this word is in us He can cause it to be like a burning passion in us. We make the Word of **God** as we believe it our own. We receive the Word and we have the very life of **Christ** in us. We become supernatural by the power of **God**. We find this power working through every part of our being by Faith

Smith Wigglesworth - JOY Unspeakable and Full of Glory

in **Christ**.

Now **Christ** gives us more than just faith. He gives us something to make faith effectual. Whatsoever you desire, if you believe in your heart you shall have. **Christ** said, **"Have faith in God. For verily I say unto you, That whosoever shall say unto this mountain, Be thou removed, and be thou cast into the sea; and shall not doubt in his heart, but shall believe that those things which he saith shall come to pass; he shall have whatsoever he saith.**

Therefore I say unto you, What things soever ye desire, when ye pray, believe that ye receive them, and ye shall have them." Mark 11:22-24. Whatsoever he saith! Dare to say in faith and it shall be done. These things have been promised by **Christ** and He can not lie.

This afflicted man stood before me helpless and withered. Cancer had filled his stomach. The physicians had operated upon him to take away the cancer from the stomach, but complications had arisen with the result that no food could enter the man's stomach. He could not swallow anything.

So in order to keep him alive they made a hole in his stomach and put in a tube about nine inches long with a cup at the top, and he was fed with liquid through this tube. For three months he had been just kept alive but had become like a skeleton.

What was I to say to him? **"If you would believe, you would see the glory of God."**

Here was the word of **Christ, "He that believes on me,**

the works that I do shall he do also, and greater works than these shall he do; because I go unto My Father." The Word of **God** is truth. **Christ** is with the Father and grants us our requests, and makes these things manifest, if we believe. What should I do in the presence of a case like this? **"Believe the Word."**

So I believed the Word which says, **"He shall have whatsoever he saith." Mark 11:23.** I said, "Go home, and have a good supper." He said, "I cannot swallow." "Go home, and have a good supper," I repeated. "On the authority of the Word of **God** I say it. **Christ** says that he that believes that these things which he says shall come to pass, he shall have whatsoever he says. So I say, Go home in the name of **Jesus**, and have a good supper."

He went home. Supper was prepared. Many times he had had food in his mouth but had always been forced to spit it out again. But I dared to believe that he would be able to swallow that night. So that man filled his mouth full as he had done before, and because someone dared to believe **God**'s Word and said to him, "You shall have a good supper in the name of **Jesus**," when he chewed his food it went down in the normal way into his stomach, and he ate until he was quite satisfied.

He and his family went to bed filled with **JOY**. The next morning when they arose they were filled with the same **JOY**. Life had begun again. Naturally he looked down to see the hole that had been made in his stomach by the physicians.

But **God** knew that he did not want two holes, and so when **God** opened the normal passage He closed the

Smith Wigglesworth - JOY Unspeakable and Full of Glory

other hole in his stomach. This is the kind of **God** we have, a **God** who knows, a **God** who acts, and brings things to pass when we believe. Dare to believe, and then dare to speak, and you shall have whatsoever you say if you doubt not.

CHAPTER EIGHT
JOY COMES BEFORE THE EVIDENCE

I learned this in 1975 as a young 19 year old Christian. Read this carefully because it holds the key to your miracle! Dr Michael H Yeager

STORY FROM SMITH WIGGLESWORTH

One day I was having a meeting in Bury, in Lancashire, England. A young woman was present who came from a place called Rams bottom, to be healed of a goiter. Before she came she said, "I am going to be healed of this goiter, mother." After one meeting she came forward and was prayed for.

The next meeting she got up and testified that she had been wonderfully healed, and she said, "I shall be so **Happy** to go and tell mother that I have been wonderfully healed." She went to her home and testified how wonderfully she had been healed, and the next year when we were having the convention she came again. To

Smith Wigglesworth - JOY Unspeakable and Full of Glory

the natural view it looked as though the goiter was just as big as ever; but that young woman was believing **God** and she was soon on her feet giving her testimony, and saying, "I was here last year and the **Lord** wonderfully healed me.

I want to tell you that this has been the best year of my life." She seemed to be greatly blessed in that meeting and she went home to testify more strongly than ever that the **Lord** had healed her. She believed **God**. The third year she was at the meeting again, and some people who looked at her said, "How big that goiter has become." But when the time came for testimony she was up on her feet and testified, "Two years ago the **Lord** graciously healed me of goiter. Oh I had a most **Wonderful** healing. It is grand to be healed by the power of **God**."

That day someone remonstrated with her and said, "People will think there is something the matter with you. Why don't you look in the glass? You will see your goiter is bigger than ever." That good woman went to the **Lord** about it and said, "**Lord**, you so wonderfully healed me two years ago. Won't you show all the people that you healed me." She went to sleep peacefully that night still believing **God** and when she came down the next day there was not a trace or a mark of that goiter.

Smith - I've never read a book but my Bible. Better to get the Book of books as food for the soul, strengthening of faith and building of character.

Not long ago I received a wire asking me if I would

go to Liverpool. There was a woman with cancer and gallstones, and she was very much discouraged. If I know **God** is sending me, my faith rises. The woman said, "I have no hope." I said, "Well, I have not come from Bradford to go home with a bad report." **God** said to me, "Establish her in the fact of the new birth."

When she had the assurance that her sin was gone and she was born again, she said, "That's everything to me. The cancer is nothing now. I have got **Jesus**." The battle was won. **God** delivered her from her sin, from her sickness, and she was free, up and dressed, and **Happy** in **Jesus**. When **God** speaks, it is as a nail in a sure place.

Will you believe, and will you receive Him? Life and immortality is ours in the gospel. This is our inheritance through the blood of **Jesus**—life for evermore!

Smith – "Always remember, the most difficult things that come to us are to our advantage from God's side."

"Not many weeks ago a lady who is a professor of music, in one of your meetings was suffering with a severe pain at the back of her neck and in her nerves. As she sat in her seat and heard you give forth the precious Word of **God**, she called on the Name of the **Lord** and was perfectly healed.

She has not had any return of the trouble. An old lady who was wonderfully healed by the **Lord** is going around as **Happy** as can be. She could scarcely walk about the

Smith Wigglesworth - JOY Unspeakable and Full of Glory

streets, now is as nimble as a child. It is beautiful to see her. You will probably remember the family in which you were used of the **Lord** in bringing husband and wife together. **God** continues to bless that family, and now four of them have received the baptism of the **Holy Spirit** according to Acts 2:4."

GODS BLESSED PRESENCE

I was traveling from Egypt to Italy. **God** was visiting me wonderfully on this ship, and every hour I was conscious of His blessed presence. A man on the ship suddenly collapsed and his wife was terribly alarmed, and everybody else was panicking. Some said that he was about to expire. But I saw it was just a glorious opportunity for the power of **God** to be manifested.

Oh, what it means to be a flame of fire, to be indwelt by the living **Christ**! We are in a bad condition if we have to pray for power when an occasion like this comes along, or if we have to wait until we feel a sense of His presence.

The **Lord**'s promise was, "Ye shall receive power after that the **Holy Ghost** is come upon you," and if we will believe, the power of **God** will be always manifested when there is a definite need. When you exercise your faith, you will find that there is the greater power in you than that is in the world. Oh, to be awakened out of unbelief into a place of daring for **God** on the authority of His blessed Book and the redemptive work of **Christ**!

So right there on board that ship, in the name of **Jesus** I rebuked the devil, and to the astonishment of the man's wife and the man himself, he was able to stand. He said, "What is this? It is going all over me. I have never felt anything like this before." From the top of his head to the soles of his feet the power of **God** shook him. **God** has given us authority over all the power of the devil. Oh, that we may live in the place where we realize this always, and that were completely submitted to that authority!

A GOOD PLACE TO BE

You are in a good place when you become sensitive to the least sin and weep before **God** about it, repenting over the least thing in which you have grieved Him. You may have spoken unkindly; you realize that it was not like the **Lord**, and your conscience has taken you to prayer. It is a **Wonderful** thing to have a sensitive conscience.

It is when we are close to **God** that our hearts are revealed to us; it is then we learn to loathe ourselves, and the **Holy Spirit** turns us to **Christ**. We take Him to be our righteousness and our holiness. **God** intends us to live in purity. He has said, **"Blessed are the pure in heart: for they shall see God."** And the pure in heart can see Him all the time in everything.

The Secret Power Of JOY

Smith Wigglesworth - JOY Unspeakable and Full of Glory

Written by Mark Hankins

But let the righteous be Glad; let them Rejoice before God: yea, let them exceedingly Rejoice. (Ps. 68:3)

...be in high spirits and glory before Him! ...glory before God, yes, let them [jubilantly] Rejoice! (Ps. 68:3 AMP)

...Oh, Rejoice in His presence. (Ps. 68:4 Living Bible)

...therefore will I offer in his tabernacle sacrifices of JOY.... (Ps. 27:6)

...sacrifices of triumphant JOY.... (Ps. 27:6 Rotherham)

Because thou hast been my help, therefore in the shadow of thy wings will I Rejoice. (Ps. 63:7)

For You have been my help, And in the shadow of Your wings I sing for JOY. (Ps. 63:7 NAB)

In Dr. Lester Sumrall's book entitled Pioneers of Faith, he gave this account of one of his personal visits with Smith Wigglesworth: One day, I asked him, "Brother Wigglesworth, how is it that you look the same every time I come? How do you feel? He bellowed at me like a bull and said, "I don't ever ask Smith Wigglesworth how he feels!"

I asked, "How do you get up in the morning?" He said, "I jump out of bed! I dance before the **Lord** for at least ten to twelve minutes - high speed dancing. I jump up and down and run around my room telling **God** how great His is, how **Glad** I am to be associated with Him and to be His child." After this, he would take a cold shower, read the Bible for an hour, then open his mail to see what **God** would have him do that day. He was an extremely remarkable man, totally sold out to **God**.

Wigglesworth was known as a man of great faith and power. Maybe it seems unusual for a man like that to get up in the morning and dance, jump, and **Rejoice** before **God**, but the supernatural signs and miracles that happened in his life were outstanding.

Apostle Paul said: Rejoice in the Lord always: and again I say, Rejoice. (Phil. 4:4)

What Happens When You Rejoice
One day, the **Lord** spoke to me so clearly and said, "If you only know what happens in the **Spirit** when you **Rejoice**, you would **Rejoice** every day.

" When we **Rejoice**, we are acting like sons and daughters of **God**! Rejoicing is an act of faith. Remember the words of Paul in Acts 27:25: "**Cheer** up..I believe **God** that it shall be as He told me." When we believe **God**, we can **Cheer** up! Believing and rejoicing ushers in the glory and goodness of **God** in our lives.

...yet believing, ye Rejoice with JOY unspeakable and full of glory.... (1 Peter 1:8)

...even now you are Happy with the inexpressible JOY that comes from heaven itself. (1 Peter 1:8 Living Bible)

Smith Wigglesworth - JOY Unspeakable and Full of Glory

JOY: The Secret of Faith And Endurance

Though the fig tree does not blossom...the fields yield no food...No cattle in the stalls, Yet I will Rejoice in the Lord...The Lord God is my Strength...He makes...me to walk...and make [spiritual] progress upon my high places [of trouble, suffering, or responsibility]! (Hab. 3:17-19 AMP)

Rejoicing will enable us to make progress in difficult times. **JOY** is the secret of faith and endurance. James 1:2 says to count it all **JOY** when trouble comes. This must be why Job laughed at destruction and trouble (Job 5:22). Of course, some people may think you are a fool, but if you have found **JOY**, you have found the secret of survival and success.

JOY's Multifaceted Connection

JOY is connected to: **God**'s presence (Ps. 16:11); **God**'s strength (Neh. 8:10); **God**'s salvation (Isa. 12:3); the anointing - the oil of **JOY** (Heb. 1:9), **God**'s medicine (Prov. 17:22); **God**'s Word (Jer. 15:16, Ps. 119:162); and prosperity (2 Cor. 9:6-10, Ps. 105:37-45).

Look at all of the blessings of **God** that are connected to **JOY**. It seems that if Satan can steal our **JOY**, then he can damage a lot of other things in our lives.

Jesus Still Laughs

JOY and rejoicing are simply a choice we make daily. It is clear that **God** did not create us to be miserable. He created us in **Christ** to enjoy life and to have dominion.

JOY is one the great secrets of faith. One of my favorite pictures of **Jesus** is the one of Him laughing triumphantly. **Jesus sits in the heavens and laughs (Ps. 2:4).** Make the choice to **Rejoice**!

Smith Wigglesworth JOY in This Life

You will show me the path of life; in Your presence is fullness of JOY; at Your right hand are pleasures forevermore. —Psalm 16:11

The Word of Life is to make your **JOY** full. We must remember that what is absent in the world is **JOY**. The world has never had **JOY**; the world never will have **JOY**. **JOY** is not in the five senses of the world. Feelings are there, happiness is there, but **JOY** can only be produced where there is no alloy. Now, there is no alloy in heaven.

Alloy means that there is a mixture. In the world there is happiness, but it is a mixture; very often it comes very close to sorrow. Often in the midst of festivities, there is a place of happiness, and right underneath is a very heavy heart. But what Christians have is this: it is **JOY** without alloy, without a mixture. It is inwardly expressive. It rises higher and higher until, if it had its perfect order, we would drown everything with a shout of praise coming from this **Holy** presence.

We want everyone to receive the **Holy Spirit** because the **Holy Spirit** has a very blessed expression of the **Lord** in

Smith Wigglesworth - JOY Unspeakable and Full of Glory

His glory, in His purity, in His power, and in all His blessed words. All these are coming forcefully through as the **Holy Spirit** is able to witness to you of Him. And every time the Son is manifested in your hearts by the **Holy Spirit**, you get a real stream of heavenly glory on earth: **JOY** in the **Holy Spirit**—not in eating and drinking, but in some-thing higher, something better.

We all enjoy eating and drinking, but this is something higher, something better, something more substantial: **JOY** in the **Holy Spirit**! And the **Holy Spirit** can bring this **JOY** to us.

Filled with the Spirit Of JOY

Do not be conformed to this world, but be transformed by the renewing of your mind, that you may prove what is that good and acceptable and perfect will of God. —Romans 12:2

God wants to make us pillars: honorable, strong, and **Holy**. **God** will move us on. I am enamored with the possibility of this. **God** wants you to know that you are saved, cleansed, delivered, and marching to victory. He has given you the faith to believe. **God** has a plan for you!

"Set your mind on things above" (Col. 3:2), and get into the heavenly places with **Christ**. You cannot repeat the name of **Jesus** too often. What a privilege it is to kneel and get right into heaven the moment we pray, where the glory descends, the fire burns, faith is active, and the light dispels the darkness. **Jesus** is the light and the life of men; no man can have this light and still walk in darkness. (See John 8:12.)

"When **Christ** who is our life appears, then you also will appear with Him in glory" (Col. 3:4). Where His life is, disease cannot remain. Is not He who dwells in us greater than all? Is He greater? Yes, when He has full control. If one thing is permitted outside the will of **God**, it hinders us in our standing against the powers of Satan. We must allow the Word of **God** to judge us, lest we stand condemned with the world (1 Cor. 11:32).

"When **Christ** who is our life appears" (Col. 3:4). Can I have any life apart from Him, any **JOY** or any fellowship apart from Him? **Jesus** said, "The ruler of this world is coming, and he has nothing in Me" (John 14:30). All that is contrary in us is withered by the indwelling life of the Son of **God**. Are we ready? Have we been clothed with the **Holy Spirit**? Has mortality been swallowed up in life? If He who is our life came, we should go.

I know that the **Lord** laid His hand on me. He filled me with the **Holy Spirit**. Heaven has begun within me. I am **Happy** now, and free, since the Comforter has come. The Comforter is the great Revealer of the kingdom of **God**. He came to give us the more abundant life. **God** has designed the plan, and nothing else really matters because the **Lord** loves us. **God** sets great store in us.

The way into glory is through the flesh being torn away

from the world and separated unto **God**. This freedom of **Spirit**, freedom from the law of sin and death, is cause for rejoicing every day. The perfect law destroys the natural law. Spiritual activity takes in every passing ray, ushering in the days of heaven upon earth, when there is no sickness and when we do not even remember that we have bodies.

The life of **God** changes us and brings us into the heavenly realm, where our reign over principalities and over all evil is limitless, powerful, and supernatural. If the natural body decays, the **Spirit** renews. Spiritual power increases until, with one mind and one heart, the glory is brought down over all the earth, right on into divine life. When the whole life is filled, this is Pentecost come again.

The life of the **Lord** will be manifested wherever we are, whether in a bus or on a train. We will be filled with the life of **Jesus** unto perfection, rejoicing in hope of the glory of **God** (Rom. 5:2), always looking for our translation into heaven.

I must have the overflowing life in the **Spirit**. **God** is not pleased with anything less. It is a disgrace to be part of an ordinary plan after we are filled with the **Holy Spirit**. We are to be salt in the earth (Matt. 5:13). We are to be hot, not lukewarm (Rev. 3:16), which means seeing **God** with eagerness, liberty, movement, and power. Believe!

*From Author Dr. Michael H Yeager
GUIDANCE

I believe with all my heart that one of the most important realities in a believer's life is that we need to hear from heaven. We need to hear directly from **God**. The Bible says:

Jeremiah 10:23 O Lord, I know that the way of man is not in himself: it is not in man that walketh to direct his steps.

Proverbs 16:25 There is a way that seemeth right unto a man, but the end thereof are the ways of death.

Now if we lean to the understanding of our mind, we will end up going down a dead end alley. The ways of the natural man will bring nothing but destruction and death. If we are not led by the **Spirit** of **God**, our life will be meaningless, having no real significance. The Scripture says:

1 Corinthians 3:19 For the wisdom of this world is foolishness with God. For it is written, He taketh the wise in their own craftiness.

If I live my life according to how I think I should live, and not according to **God's** will, **God's** plan, **God's** purposes for my life, it will end up being nothing but a waste of time. What's going to happen after I die and stand before the **Lord** if I have lived my life this way? I will find out that everything I did in this world had no meaning and had no real significance.

I know I'm specifically speaking to believers, but this is even more frightening. I think most people who call themselves believers are living lives that have no meaning and no significance. What I mean by this statement is that when you stand before **God**, and you give an account of your life, but you have lived your life the way you wanted, you will have nothing to offer to **God**.

Smith Wigglesworth - JOY Unspeakable and Full of Glory

When the disciples looked at **Jesus**, they saw something different about his life. That's why they said to him: **Lord** teach us to pray! As believers there's should be something different about our lives, every step, every word, and everything we do. Listen to the amazing response that **Jesus** gave his disciples.

Matthew 6:9 After this manner therefore pray ye: Our Father which art in heaven, Hallowed be thy name. 10 Thy KINGDOM come, Thy will be done in earth, as it is in heaven.

The foundation of a believer's life is this: **I want your will Father to be done in my life today, and every day, in every area.** Now notice it's a day by day walk. Sometimes, most times for me it's a minute by minute situation. I want Gods will to be done for me today, right now on earth as it is in heaven. If you really do not care about the will of **God**, then what I'm saying is going to go right over the top of your head.

Most believers I have known are more interested in talking about football, NASCAR, politics and the weather. Most likely you are not in this category, because you have taken the time to purchase this book, and to read it.

Now, I use to be really deep into hunting and fishing, sports, but when I experienced the reality of **Jesus Christ**, all of these things became extremely boring to me. When I hear somebody talk about **Jesus**, then my ears perk up. I want to stop and listen. I want to see what you have to say because that's what I'm looking for. I'm looking for the will of **God** to be done in my life as it is in heaven.

CHAPTER NINE
APPREHENDED BY GOD

I feel somehow that my heart is very much enlarged, that my COMPASSION for my **Lord** is intensified, that nothing is too hard. The people in the days of the apostles took joyfully the spoiling of their goods, [He 10.34] and I feel there is a measure of grace given to the man who says, "I will go all the way with **Jesus**." What is that measure of grace?

It is a girding with hopefulness in pressing forward to the goal that **God** would have us reach. But it is important that we forget not Paul's words, "Let no man take thy crown." [Rv 3.11] He saw there was a possibility lest any man who had been the means of sowing the good seed of the gospel should lose that for which **God** had apprehended him.

A Life Filled with JOYFULNESS

Smith Wigglesworth - JOY Unspeakable and Full of Glory

"That I may know Him, and the power of His resurrection, and the fellowship of His sufferings, being made conformable unto His death... I count not myself to have apprehended; but this one thing I do, forgetting those things which are behind, and reaching forth unto those things which are before, I press toward the mark for the prize of the high calling of **God** in **Christ Jesus**." Philippians 3:10-14.

What a **Wonderful** word! This surely means to press on to be filled with all the fullness of **God**. If we leak out here we shall surely miss **God**, and shall fail in fulfilling the ministry He would give us.

The **Lord** would have us preach by life, and by deed, always abounding in service; living epistles, bringing forth to men the knowledge of **God**. If we went all the way with **God**, what would happen? What should we see if we would only seek to bring honor to the name of our **God**? Here we see Paul pressing in for this. There is no standing still. We must move on to a fuller power of the **Spirit**, never satisfied that we have apprehended all, but filled with the assurance that **God** will take us on to the goal we desire to reach, as we press on for the prize ahead.

Abraham came out from Ur of the Chaldees. We never get into a new place until we come out from the old one. There is a place where we leave the old life behind, and where the life in **Christ** fills us and we are filled with His glorious personality.

On the road to Damascus, Saul of Tarsus was apprehended by **Christ**. From the first he sent up a cry, "**Lord**, what wilt thou have me to do?" He desired always to do the will of **God**, but here he realized a place of closer intimacy, a place of fuller power, of deeper crucifixion. He sees a prize ahead and every fiber of his being is intent on securing that prize. **Jesus Christ** came to be the firstfruits; the firstfruits of a great harvest of like fruit, like unto Himself. How zealous is the farmer as he watches his crops and sees the first shoots and blades. They are the earnest of the great harvest that is coming. Paul here is longing that the Father's heart shall be satisfied, for in that first resurrection the Heavenly Husbandman will see a firstfruits harvest, firstfruits like unto **Christ**, sons of **God** made conformable to the only begotten Son of **God**

You say, "I am in a needy place." It is in needy places that **God** delights to work. For three days the people that were with **Christ** were without food, and He asked Philip, "From whence shall we buy bread that these may eat?" That was a hard place for Philip, but not for **Jesus**, for He knew perfectly what He would do. The hard place is where He delights to show forth His miraculous power. And haw fully was the need provided for. Bread enough and to spare!

Two troubled, baffled travelers are on the road to Emmaus. As they communed together and reasoned, **Jesus** Himself drew near, and He opened up the Word to them in such a way that they saw light in His light. Their eyes were holden that they could not recognize who it was talking with them. But, o how their hearts burned within as He opened up the Scripture to them. And at the breaking of bread He was made known to them. Always seek to be found in the place where He manifests His presence and power.

The resurrected **Christ** appeared to Peter and a few more of them early one morning on the shore of the lake. He prepared a meal for the tired, tried disciples. That is just like Him. Count on His presence. Count on His power. Count on His provision. He is always there just where you need Him.

Have you received Him? Are you to be found "in Him"? Have you received His righteousness, which is by faith? Abraham got to this place, for **God** gave this righteousness to him because he believed, and as you believe **God** He puts HIs righteousness to your account. He will put His righteousness right within you. He will keep you in perfect peace as you stay your mind upon Him and trust in Him. He will bring you to a rest of faith, to a place of blessed assurance that all that happens is working for your eternal good.

Here is the widow's son on the road to burial. **Jesus** meets that

Smith Wigglesworth - JOY Unspeakable and Full of Glory

unhappy procession. He has COMPASSION on that poor woman who is taking her only son to the cemetery. His great heart had such COMPASSION that death had no power—it could no longer hold its prey. COMPASSION is greater than suffering. COMPASSION is greater than death. O **God**, give us this COMPASSION! In His infinite COMPASSION **Jesus** stopped that funeral procession and cried to that widow's son, "Young man, I say unto thee, Arise." And he who was dead sat up, and **Jesus** delivered him to his mother.

Paul got a vision and revelation of the resurrection power of **Christ**, and so he was saying, "I will not stop until I have laid hold of what **God** has laid hold of me for." For what purpose has **God** laid hold of us? To be channels for His power. He wants to manifest the power of the Son of **God** through you and me. **God** help us to manifest the faith of **Christ**, the COMPASSION of **Christ**, the resurrection power of **Christ**.

One morning about eleven o'clock I saw a woman who was suffering with tumor. She could not live through the day. A little blind girl led me to the bedside. COMPASSION broke me up and I wanted that woman to live for the child's sake. I said to the woman, "Do you want to live?" She could not speak. She just moved her finger. I anointed her with oil and said, "In the name of **Jesus**." There was a stillness of death that followed; and the pastor, looking at the woman, said to me, "She is gone."

When **God** pours in His COMPASSION it has resurrection power in it. I carried that woman across the room, put her against a wardrobe and held her there. I said, "In the name of **Jesus**, death come out." And soon her body began to tremble like a leaf. "In **Jesus**' name, walk," I said. She did and went back to bed.

I told this story in the assembly. There was a doctor there and he said, "I'll prove that." He went to the woman and she told him it was perfectly true. She said, "I was in heaven, and I saw countless numbers all like **Jesus**. Then I heard a voice saying, 'Walk, in the name of **Jesus**.' "

There is power in the name of **Jesus**. Let us apprehend it, the power of His resurrection, the power of His COMPASSION, the power of His love. Love will break the hardest thing—there is nothing it will not break.

We Have a Big God.

We have a **Wonderful Jesus**. We have a glorious Comforter. **God**'s canopy is over you and will cover you at all times, preserving you from evil. Under His wings shalt thou trust. The Word of **God** is living and powerful and in its treasures you will find eternal life. If you dare trust this **Wonderful Lord**, this **Lord** of life, you will find in Him everything you need.

So many are tampering with drugs, quacks, pills and plasters. Clear them all out and believe **God**. It is sufficient to believe **God**. You will find that if you dare trust Him, He will never fail. "The prayer of faith shall save the sick, and the **LORD**.

He is a big **Jesus**! If I could measure Him I would be very small. But I cannot measure Him, and I know He is very large. I am **Glad** I cannot measure **Jesus** but I am **Glad** I can touch Him all the same. The fifth verse: One **Lord**, one faith, one baptism. Ephesians 4:5.

I must touch the thought of baptism this morning. We must get away from the thought of water baptism when we are in the epistles. If water baptism is at all mentioned in any way, it is always mentioned as a past tense.

We must always remember this, beloved, that while water baptism, in my opinion, is essential, "He that believeth, and is baptized, shall be saved." I wouldn't say for a moment a man could not be saved without he was baptized in water, because it would be contrary to Scripture. Yet I see there is a blending. If we turn to the third chapter of John's gospel we find:

Smith Wigglesworth - JOY Unspeakable and Full of Glory

...Except a man be born of water and of the **Spirit**, he cannot enter into the KINGDOM of **God**. John 3:5b

I believe **God** would have us to know that we never ought to put aside water baptism, but believe it is in perfect conjunction and in operation with the working of the **Spirit** that we may be buried with Him.

WHAT MAKES YOU HAPPY?

You shall receive power when the Holy Spirit has come upon you. —Acts 1:8

My friend, you need a double cure. You first need saving and cleansing and then the baptism of the **Holy Spirit**, until the old man never rises anymore, until you are absolutely dead to sin and alive to **God** by His **Spirit** and know that old things have passed away.

When the **Holy Spirit** gets possession of a person, he is a new being entirely—he becomes saturated with divine power. We become a habitation of Him who is all light, all revelation, all power, and all love. Yes, **God** the **Holy Spirit** is manifested within us in such a way that it is glorious. A certain rich man in London had a flourishing business.

He used to count his many assets, but he was still troubled inside; he didn't know what to do. Walking around his large building, he came upon a boy who was the doorkeeper; he found the boy whistling. Looking at him, he sized up the whole situation completely and went back to his office again and puzzled over the matter.

Although he continued with his business, he could find no peace. His bank could not help him; his money, his success, could not help him. He had an aching void. He was helpless within. My friend, having the world without having **God** is like being "whitewashed tombs" (Matt. 23:27). When he could get no rest, he exclaimed, —I will go and see what the boy is doing.‖ Again he went and found him whistling. —I want you to come into my office,‖ he said.

When they entered the office, the man said, —Tell me, what makes you so **Happy** and **Cheerful**?‖ —Oh,‖ replied the boy, —I used to be so miserable until I went to a little mission and heard about **Jesus**. Then I was saved and filled with the **Holy Spirit**. I am always whistling inside; if I am not whistling, I am singing. I am just full!‖ This rich man obtained the address of the mission from the boy, went to the services, and sat near the door.

But the power of **God** moved so strongly that when the altar call was given, he responded. **God** saved him and, a few days afterward, filled him with the **Holy Spirit**. The man found himself at his desk, shouting, —Oh, **Hallellujah**!‖ The blessed Son of **God** wants to fill us with such glory until our whole body is aflame with the power of the **Holy Spirit**. I see there is "much more" (Rom. 5:9).

My daughter asked some African boys to tell her the difference between being saved and being filled with the

Smith Wigglesworth - JOY Unspeakable and Full of Glory

Holy Spirit. —Ah,‖ they said, —when we were saved, it was very good; but when we received the **Holy Spirit**, it was more so.‖ Many of you have never received the —more so.‖ After the **Holy Spirit** comes upon you, you will have power. **God** will mightily move within your life; the power of the **Holy Spirit** will overshadow you, inwardly moving you until you know there is a divine plan different from anything that you have had in your life before.

Has He come? He is going to come to you. I am expecting that **God** will so manifest His presence and power that He will show you the necessity of receiving the **Holy Spirit**. Also, **God** will heal those who need healing. Everything is to be had now: salvation, sanctification, the fullness of the **Holy Spirit**, and healing. **God** is working mightily by the power of His **Spirit**, bringing to us a fullness of His perfect redemption until every soul may know that **God** has all power.

State your Position in God

Smith - Voice your position in God and you will be surrounded by all the resources of God in the time of trial.

There are many that say they are believers but they are full of sickness and do not take a hold of the life of the **Lord Jesus Christ** that is provided for them. I was taken to see a woman who was dying and said to her, "How are you doing spiritually?"

`She answered, "I have faith, I believe." I said, "You know that you do not have faith, you know that you are dying. It is not faith that you have, it is mere mental acknowledgment." There is a difference between knowing something in your head and having faith. I saw that she was in the influence of the devil.

There was no possibility of divine life until the enemy was removed from the premises. I hate the devil, and I laid hold of the woman and shouted, "Come out, you devil of death. I command you to come out in the name of **Jesus**." In one minute she stood on her feet in completely healed and in victory.

Remember God's Goodness

In all your ways acknowledge Him, and He shall direct your paths.—Proverbs 3:6

After **Jesus** had departed from the Pharisees, He said to His disciples, "Take heed and beware of the leaven of the Pharisees and the Sadducees" (Matt. 16:6). The disciples began to discuss this warning among themselves, and all they could think of was that they had brought no bread. What were they going to do? Then **Jesus** uttered these words: "O you of little faith"

He had been with them for quite a while, yet they were still a great disappointment to Him because of their lack of comprehension and of faith. They could not grasp the profound spiritual truth He was bringing to them and could only think about having brought no bread. So **Jesus** said to them, **O you of little faith…Do you not yet understand, or remember the five loaves of the five thousand and how many baskets you took up?**

Smith Wigglesworth - JOY Unspeakable and Full of Glory

Nor the seven loaves of the four thousand and how many large baskets you took up? (Matt. 16:8–10)

Do you keep in mind how **God** has been gracious in the past? **God** has done **Wonderful** things for all of us. If we keep these things in mind, we will be "strengthened in [our] faith" (Rom. 4:20). We should be able to defy Satan in everything. Remember that the **Lord** has led all the way.

When Joshua passed over the Jordan on dry land, he told the people to pick up twelve stones and set them up in Gilgal. These were to be a constant reminder to the children of Israel that they came over the Jordan on dry land. (See Joshua 4:20–24.) How many times had **Jesus** shown His disciples the mightiness of His power? Yet they failed in faith right here.

Better Day by Day

Put on the whole armor of God, that you may be able to stand against the wiles of the devil. —Ephesians 6:11

I am more and more convinced every day I live that very few who are saved by the grace of **God** have a right conception of how great their authority is over darkness, demons, death, and every power of the Enemy. It is a real **JOY** when we realize our inheritance.

I was speaking like this one day, and someone said, I have never heard anything like this before. How many months did it take you to think up that sermon? I said, My brother, **God** pressed my wife from time to time to get me to preach, and I promised her I would preach. I used to labor hard for a week to think something up, then give out the text and sit down and say, I am done.' Oh, brother, I have given up thinking things up. They all come down. And the sermons that come down, stop down, then go back, because the Word of **God** says His Word will not return to Him void (Isa. 55:11).

If you get anything up in your own power, it will not stay up very long; when it goes down, it will take you down with it. The sons of **God** are made manifest in this present earth to destroy the power of the Devil. To be saved by the power of **God** is to be brought from the realm of the ordinary into the extraordinary, from the natural into the divine.

Do you remember the day when the **Lord** laid His hands on you? You say, I could not do anything except praise the **Lord**. Well, that was only the beginning. Where are you today? The divine plan is that you increase until you receive the measureless fullness of **God**. You do not have to say, I tell you it was **Wonderful** when I was baptized with the **Holy Spirit**. If you have to look back to the past to make me know you are baptized, then you are back-slidden.

If the beginning was good, it ought to be better day by day, until everybody is fully convinced that you are filled

Smith Wigglesworth - JOY Unspeakable and Full of Glory

with the might of **God** in the **Spirit**, "filled with all the fullness of **God**" (Eph. 3:19). "Do not be drunk with wine, in which is dissipation; but be filled with the **Spirit**" (Eph. 5:18). I don't want anything other than being full and fuller and fuller, until I am overflowing like a great big vat. Do you realize that if you have been created anew and born again by the Word of **God** that there is within you the word of power and the same light and life as the Son of **God** Himself had?

God wants to flow through you with measureless power of divine utterance and grace until your whole body is a flame of fire. So many people have been baptized with the **Holy Spirit**; there was a movement, but they have become monuments, and you cannot move them. **God**, wake us out of sleep lest we should become indifferent to the glorious truth and the breath of Your almighty power.

We must be the light and salt of the earth (Matt. 5:13–14), with the whole armor of **God** upon us (Eph. 6:11). It would be a serious thing if the enemies were about and we had to go back and get our shoes. It would be a serious thing if we had on no breastplate. How can we be furnished with the armor? Take it by faith. Jump in, stop in, and never come out, for this is a baptism to be lost in, where you only know one thing and that is the desire of **God** at all times.

The baptism in the **Spirit** should be an ever increasing endowment of power, an ever increasing enlargement of grace. Oh, Father, grant us a real look into the glorious liberty You have designed for the children of **God**, who

169

are delivered from this present world, separated, sanctified, and made suitable for Your use, whom You have designed to be filled with all Your fullness.

We Have a God of Love

It is a most blessed thought that we have a **God** of love, of COMPASSION, and of grace, who willeth not the death of one sinner. **God** has made it possible for all men to be saved, by causing **Jesus**, His well-beloved Son, to die for the sins of the whole world. It is true that He took our sins; it is true that He paid the price for the whole world; it is true that He gave Himself a ransom for many; it is true, beloved, it is true. And you say, "For whom?"

"Whosoever will, let him take the water of life freely." What about the others? It would have to be a refusal of the Blood of **Jesus**; it would have to be a refusal to have **Christ** reign over them; that's it. It is "Whosoever will," on the one side, and "Whosoever won't" on the other side; and there are people in the world who "won't." What is up with them? "The **God** of this world hath blinded the minds of them that believed not, lest the light of the glorious gospel of **Christ**, who is the image of **God**, should shine unto them."

Through sanctification of the **Spirit**, according to this election, you will get to a place where you are not disturbed. There is a peace in the sanctification of the **Spirit**, because it is a place of revelation—of heavenly places into which you are brought. It is a place where **God** comes and makes Himself known unto you; and when You are face to face with **God** you get a peace that passes all understanding, and which lifts you from state to state of inexpressible wonderment. Oh, it is **Wonderful!**

"Blessed be the **God** and Father of our **Lord Jesus Christ**, which according to His abundant mercy, hath begotten us again unto a

Smith Wigglesworth - JOY Unspeakable and Full of Glory

lively hope by the resurrection of **Jesus Christ** from the dead."
This sanctification of the **Spirit** brings us into definite line with
this **Wonderful** "lively hope" of the glory of **God**.

A lively hope is exactly the opposite of something dead. A lively
hope means movement. A lively hope means looking into what we
hope for. A lively hope means pressing into that which is
promised. A lively hope means leaving behind you other things. A
lively hope means keeping the vision. A lively hope sees **Jesus**
coming.

And you live in this lively hope. You are not trying to make
yourself feel that you are believing. But this lively hope keeps you
waiting, and ready, and filled with the **JOY** of expectation of the
coming of the King. Praise the **Lord**! If the thought of the coming
of the King is not such a lively hope to you, you need to search
whether you have ever truly enthroned Him as King over your own
life. **God** has this in mind for you. There is real **JOY** in
expectation of His coming; and there will be infinitely greater **JOY**
in the realization.

I trust that you will be so reconciled to **God** that not one thing will
interfere with your having this lively hope. If you have any love
for the world, this hope cannot be a lively hope to you; for His
coming will mean the overthrow of the world. If there is in you the
pride of life, this hope cannot be to you a lively hope; for every
high thing will be brought low in that day.

Salvation is very much misunderstood. That which comes to you in
a moment of time, through believing, is only the beginning,
Salvation is so **Wonderful**, so mighty, so tremendous, that it goes
on and on from one degree to another until there shall be nothing
in us from which we need to be delivered, either in **Spirit**, or soul,
or mind, or body, Everything is ready so far as **God** is concerned,
and is waiting for man to get ready to receive it.

Sin began in the soul of man, and salvation must be wrought out
there before there can be deliverance from the consequences of sin.
In the meantime, if we rest our faith in the power of **God**, we will
be "kept by the power of **God** through faith unto salvation ready to

be revealed in the last time."

You have no idea what **God** wants to do for you through trials and temptations. They do two things for us: Where there is anything wrong in us which we are not recognizing, they bring it to the surface, that we may see our need of **God**'s salvation in this respect.

But why are the most faithful also of **God**'s children tried and tempted? It is that their very faithfulness and loyalty and the purity of their faith may be MADE MANIFEST, and "found unto praise and honor and glory at the appearing of **Jesus Christ**." Gold has to he tried with fire, and it is made more precious thereby. Your faith, Peter says, "is MUCH MORE PRECIOUS than gold that perisheth."

Jumping and Leaping and Praising God

Our dear Brother Wigglesworth arrived in Melbourne last Thursday, February 16th, Amongst those who came forward for prayer were several who declared that they had received remarkable and instantaneous healings. A few of those were as follows: One little girl, six years of age, was seen, after prayer by the evangelist, walking out of the front door of the building with her mother, who was delightedly exclaiming to all and sundry, "Look at her!

She has never walked in her life before!" A man who had not walked for over four years owing to rheumatoid arthritis, was instantly healed, and after triumphantly passing his stick and crutch up to the platform, gave an

Smith Wigglesworth - JOY Unspeakable and Full of Glory

impromptu exhibition of the power that had come into his legs by jumping and leaping and praising **God**.

Others suffering from weak spine, nerve and heart trouble, weak eyesight, asthma, kidney trouble, loss of voice, etc., claimed to have been wonderfully helped.

Since the first night there have been many other **Wonderful** healings. Last night a dear woman who had been unable to walk for 61 years was brought to be prayed for, and—glory be to **God**!—she got out of her chair and walked, and her husband pushed her chair along, with her walking behind. Praise our covenant-keeping **God**! Truly He is able to do exceeding abundantly above all that we can ask or think.

There have also been many conversions—at one meeting alone 40 dear ones accepted **Jesus** as their **Lord** and Savior—and we are believing for still greater things. The revival showers are falling and **God** is working. Bless His **Holy** Name!

Just this morning a mother brought her little girl along, who had fallen on a pair of scissors, and cut her mouth so that she could not close it. After the evangelist had laid his hands upon it and prayed, she was able to close her mouth and was quite well. Glory to **God**!

Secret of His Power.

A dear young Russian came to England. He did not know the language, but learned it quickly and was very much used and blessed of **God**; and as the **Wonderful** manifestations of the power of **God** were seen, they pressed upon him to know the secret of his power.

He felt it was so sacred between him and **God** he should not tell it, but they pressed him so much he finally said to them: "First **God** called me, and His presence was so precious, that I said to **God** at every call I would obey Him, and I yielded, and yielded, and yielded, until I realized that I was simply clothed with another power altogether, and I realized that **God** took me, tongue, thoughts and everything, and I was not myself but it was **Christ** working through me."

How many of you today have known that **God** has called you over and over, and has put His hand upon you, but you have not yielded in every area of your life? How many of you have had the breathing of His power within you, calling you to prayer, or the meditation of the word and you have to confess you have failed?

She Laughed Heartily

Last night a large number of persons came "for aid," to use the evangelist's expression; and though he was not successful in all cases, there; were many in which there appeared to be startling and immediate improvement after he had laid his; hands on the afflicted and prayed over them.

In one instance a woman who was said to have been very deaf was able to answer him when he spoke to her in an ordinary tone. In another an elderly man, who declared that he had suffered from; noises in the head for ten years, said that he was free from them at last. An elderly woman who was described as almost crippled with rheumatism, was directed to stoop down and touch the ground with her hands. "I don't suppose you have bent your back for some time," Mr. Wigglesworth said.

The patient stooped down without effort! Apparently, and was so delighted that she laughed heartily. "No pain and no stiffness now?" asked the evangelist, and she replied that she had none. A girl who had an affliction of the hip and knee, which it was said had prevented her walking without a stick for some years, walked up and down to front of the audience at a rapid pace, whereas she had only been able before to limp slowly with the aid of her stick. "Throw your stick away; burn it," said Mr. Wigglesworth. "You will not want it again." Many other cases gave interesting results.

A Man of Longsuffering

The man who is going through with **God** to be used in healing must be a man of longsuffering. He must be always ready with a word of comfort. If the sick one is in distress and helpless and does not see everything eye to eye with you, you must bear with him. Our **Lord** Tesus **Christ** was filled with COMPASSION and lived and moved in a place of longsuffering, and we will have to get into this place if we are to help needy ones.

There are some times when you pray for the sick and you are apparently rough. But you are not dealing with a person, you are dealing with the Satanic forces that are binding the person.

Your heart is full of love and COMPASSION to all, but you are moved to a **Holy** anger as you see the place the devil has taken in the body of the sick one, and you deal with his position with a real forcefulness. One day a pet dog followed a lady out of her house and ran all round her feet.

She said to the dog, "My dear, I cannot have you with me today." The dog wagged its tail and made a big fuss. She said, "Go home, my dear." But the dog did not go. At last she shouted roughly, "Go home," and off it went. Some people deal with the devil like that, The devil can stand all the comfort you like to give him. Cast him out!

You are dealing not with the person, you are dealing with the devil. Demon power must be dislodged in the name of the **Lord**. You are always right when you dare to deal with sickness as with the devil. Much sickness is caused by some misconduct, there is something wrong, there is some neglect somewhere, and Satan has had a chance to get in. It is necessary to repent and confess where you have given place to the devil, and then he can be dealt with.

CHAPTER TEN

THE WORLD HATH HATED THEM

Published in the Pentecostal Evangel, May 30, 1925.

Whenever, in the history of the world, there has been a divine revelation, **God** coming forth in some manifestation of His **Spirit**, there have been antagonism and opposition to the same with persecution of those who received such manifestations or revelations. In the old dispensation, as well as in the new, when the **Spirit** of **God** has been moving mightily, there has been trouble and difficulty.

Why is this? It is because there are some things very much against revelation of **God** and the operation of the **Spirit** of **God**. First, there is the flesh, the natural man, because, "The carnal mind is enmity against **God**." The very fact that men throughout the world, as a rule, are opposed to the working of **God**, is evidence of the truth of this statement of Scripture.

Out of this enmity of the mind of the natural man against **God** grows the opposition of the world, which is the mass of these antagonistic individuals. Our **Lord Jesus Christ** has made it unmistakably plain to all His followers for all time that the world is contrary to Him and to His KINGDOM. He said concerning His disciples, "I have given them thy word; and THE WORLD HATH HATED THEM, because they are not of the world, even as I am not of the world."

The devil and all his evil hosts are also arrayed against all manifestations of **God**. The devil is "the prince of this world;" and he is "the **Spirit** that now worketh in the children of disobedience." All these are opposed to **God** and His working; but they can never defeat the purposes of **God**.

So far as the human eye can see, **God**'s cause is often in the minority; but viewed by those who have spiritual eyesight. "They that be with us are more than they that be with them." So, as Elisha said to his servant, "Fear not." Wickedness may increase and abound; but when the **Lord** raises His banner over the saint, it is victory, though the saint may seem to be in the minority.

So we read in the first verse that these saints were "scattered abroad," meaning that they did not have much liberty to meet together, but were driven from place to place. In the days of John Knox of Scotland the people who served **God** had to be in very close quarters, because the Roman church set out to destroy them. They were in the minority from the human viewpoint, but they swept through to victory, and the Roman power was defeated in Scotland. Cry to **God** that it may not rise again, for it has always meant bloodshed to the saints of **God** and opposition to the working of the **Holy Ghost**.

The **Holy Ghost** wants us to understand our privileges—"elect according to the foreknowledge of **God** the Father, through sanctification of the **Spirit**." This work of the sanctification of the **Spirit** does not refer to cleansing from sin. It refers to a higher order of redemptive work. The blood of **Jesus** is all-powerful for cleansing; but when sin is gone, when we are clean and when we know we have the Word of **God** in us, and when the power of the **Spirit** is bringing everything to a place where we triumph over all evil, then comes a revelation through the **Spirit** which lifts you on to higher ground and unveils the fullness of the life of **Christ** within us in such a way that we are led on till we are "FILLED unto all the FULNESS of **God**."

Smith Wigglesworth - JOY Unspeakable and Full of Glory

This is the sanctification of the **Spirit**. It is the great work for which the **Spirit** is given. This is the purpose for which **God** has called you; but whether you have accepted your election, whether you proved yourself worthy of your election, whether you have allowed this **Spirit** to thus sanctify you, I do not know; but if you yield yourself to **God** and let His **Holy Spirit** have His way in your **Spirit** to lead you into the will of **God**, as it is revealed in the Word of **God**, He will not fail to "do exceeding abundantly above all that we ask or think."

This word "elect" is a very precious word to me. It shows me that, before the world was, **God** planned to bring us into such glorious triumph and victory in **Christ** that "unto him (shall) be the glory in the church by **Christ Jesus** throughout all ages, world without end. Amen." Feed upon these words. Let them sink into your heart— **God** has purposed to do for those in the church something which will redound to the glory of His Name unto the endless ages. This is the most solid ground for faith—that salvation is to be "to the praise of the glory of His grace." **God** has predetermined, has planned, has made full provision to accomplish this wondrous work in all who will not "frustrate the grace of **God**."

Some people pervert this blessed truth; they say, "Oh, well, you see, we are elected; we are all right." I know many who believe in that kind of election. They say they are elected to be saved; and they believe others are elected to be damned. It is not true. Everybody is elected to be saved; whether they come into it or not is another thing.

This perverted view of this precious truth makes souls indifferent to its great purpose, the "sanctification of the **Spirit**." This is one of the ways in which Satan opposes the work of **God** in the world—by perverting it, making it to appear to mean something that it does not mean; so that souls are kept from pressing on into the glorious purpose of **God** for which salvation was planned. That would be a poor salvation which did not deliver man from the thing which causes all the sorrow and trouble in this world—SIN.

Notice again, this sanctification of the **Spirit** is "unto obedience and sprinkling of the blood of **Jesus Christ**." There is no sanctification if it is not sanctification unto obedience. There would be no trouble with any of us if we would all come definitely to the place where we understand and accept that Word of our **Lord Jesus** when He said, "For their sakes I sanctify myself, that they also might be sanctified through the truth.

Sanctify them through thy truth; thy word is truth." When you come into the election of the sanctification of the **Spirit**, you will be obedient to everything revealed in that Word; and in the measure that you are not obedient you have not come into the sanctification of the **Spirit**.

A little thing spoils many good things. People say, "Mrs. So-and-So is very good, but—" "Oh, you know that young man is progressing tremendously, but—" There are no "buts" in the sanctification of the **Spirit**. "But" and "if" are gone, and it is "shall" and "I will" all the way through. Beloved, if there are any "buts" in your attitude toward the Word of Truth, it indicates that there is something unyielded to the **Spirit**. I do pray **God** that we may be willing to yield ourselves to the sanctification of the **Spirit**, that we may enter into the mind of **God** regarding this election, in actual possession of it.

Perhaps to encourage you, it will be helpful to show you what election is; because there is no difficulty in proving whether you are elected or not. Why are you interested in this book? Is it because you have a desire for more of **God**? If so, it is **God** who has given you that desire; and **God** is drawing you unto Himself.

If you have truly received **Jesus** as your **Lord** and Savior, it has been because the Father drew you to Him; for He said, "No man can come to me, except the Father which hath sent me draw him." And we may be sure that **God** will not go back on what He has begun to do; for our **Lord Jesus** added to the above, "And I will raise him up at the last day." Also the apostle Paul says, in Philippians 1:6, "Being confident of this very thing, that he which hath begun a good work in you will perform it until the day of **Jesus Christ**."

Smith Wigglesworth - JOY Unspeakable and Full of Glory

One day I went to a certain place and a gentleman there said to me, "Would you like to see the purification of gold?" I replied, "Yes." So he got some gold and put it into a crucible, and put a blast of heat under it. First it became blood red, and then changed and changed. Then this man took an instrument and passed it over the gold. It drew off something, which was foreign to the gold. He did this several times, until every bit of that foreign substance was taken away. Then he said to me, "Look!" And there we both saw our faces in the gold! It was **Wonderful**!

My brother, the trial of your faith is much more precious than of gold that perisheth. As you are tested in the fire, the Master is bringing the dross to the surface, that He may take it away, all that hinders His image being seen in you—taking away all the dross from your life, all that is not enduring, all that is not precious in His sight.

It is lovely to know that, in times of misunderstanding, times when you are in the right and yet are treated as though you were in the wrong, **God** is meeting you, blessing you, accomplishing something which will not only glorify His name, but be to your "praise and honor and glory at the appearing of **Jesus Christ**." So do not chafe or fret; let the fire burn; it will do you good.

Love and COMPASSION for All

I come to you with a great inward desire to wake you up to your great possibilities. Your responsibilities will be great, but not as great as your possibilities. You will always find that **God** is over-abundance on every line he touches for you, and he wants you to come into mind and thought with him so that you are not straightened in yourselves. Be enlarged in **God**!

[Tongues and interpretation. "It is that which **God** hath chosen for us, which is mightier than we. It is that which is bottomless, higher than the heights, more lovely than all beside. And **God** in a measure presses you out to believe all things that you may endure ail things, and lay hold of eternal life through the power of the **Spirit**."]

The "gifts of healings" are **Wonderful** gifts. There is a difference between having a gift of healing, and "gifts of healings." **God** wants us not to come behind in anything. I like this word, "gifts of healing." To have the accomplishment of these gifts I must bring myself to a conformity to the mind and will of **God** in purpose. It would be impossible to have "gifts of healing" unless you possessed that blessed fruit of "longsuffering." You will find these gifts run parallel with that which will bring them into operation without a leak.

But how will it be possible to minister the gifts of healing, considering the peculiarities there are in the Assemblies, and the many evil powers of Satan which confront us and possess bodies? The man who will go through with **God** and exercise the gifts of healing will have to be a man of longsuffering; always have a word of comfort. If the one who is in distress and helpless doesn't see eye to eye in everything, and doesn't get all he wants, longsuffering will bear and forbear. Longsuffering is a grace **Jesus** lived in and moved in. He was filled with COMPASSION, and **God** will never be able to move us to the help of the needy one till we reach that place.

Sometimes you might think by the way I went about praying for the sick that I was unloving and rough; but oh friends, you have no idea what I see behind the sickness and the afflicted. I am not dealing with the person; I am dealing with the satanic forces that are binding the afflicted. As far as the person goes, my heart is full of love and COMPASSION for all, but I fail to see how you will ever reach a place where **God** will be able definitely to use you until you get angry at the devil.

If you say, with authority, "Come out, you demons, in the name of the **Lord**!" they must come out. You will always be right when you dare to treat sickness as the devil's work and you will always be near the mark when you treat it as sin. Let Pentecostal people wake up to see that getting sick is caused by some misconduct; there is some neglect, something wrong somewhere, a weak place where Satan has had a chance to get in. And if we wake up to the real facts of it, we will be ashamed to say that we are sick because people will know we have been sinning.

"Unity of the Spirit"

Endeavoring to keep the unity of the Spirit in the bond of peace.

--Ephesians 4:3

Scripture reading: **Psalm 133**

You are bound forever out of loyalty to **God** to see that no division comes into the church body, to see that nothing comes into the assembly, as it came into David's flock, to tear and rend the body. You have to be careful. If a person comes along with a prophecy and you find that it is tearing down and bringing trouble, denounce it accordingly; judge it by the Word.

You will find that all true prophecy will be perfectly full of hopefulness. It will have COMPASSION; it will have comfort; it will have edification. So if anything comes into the church that you know is hurting the flock and disturbing the assembly, you must see to it that you begin to pray so that this thing is put to death.

Bring unity in the bonds of perfection so that the church of **God** will receive edification. Then the church will begin to be built up in the faith and the establishing of truth, and believers will be one. There is one body. Recognize that fact. When schism comes into the body, believers always act as though there were more than one body.

Do not forget that **God** means for us to be very faithful to the church so that we do not allow anything to come into the church to break up the body. You cannot find anything in the body in its relation to **Christ** that has schism in it.

Christ's life in the body--there is not schism in that. When **Christ**'s life comes into the church, there will be no discord; there will be perfect blending of heart and hand, and it will be lovely. Endeavor "to keep the unity of the **Spirit** in the bond of peace."

Thought for today: When we think that the church is poor and needy, we forget that the **Spirit** of intercession can unlock every safe in the world.

Perfect Liberty of God

We are Looking into the perfect liberty of **God** where we have the unfolding of the majesty of heaven. Where **Christ** is so revealed in all his divine fullness that we see from the beginning to the end one ideal through the whole canon of the scriptures.

God hath set him over all. And **God** is manifesting in us himself, for in us all this truth has to be, and the truth is that we should know the scriptures which make us wise unto salvation; [2Ti 3.15] which open the depths of the KINGDOM of heaven.

He reveals all his divine mind to us; [1Co 2.10] which strengtheneth by the might of his **Spirit** in the inner man [Ep 3.16] till the whole man is changed. The mysteries are by the **Spirit** revealed unto us and we know that **God** is bringing us into this glorious fact of having the mind of **Christ** and the knowledge of **God**.

Smith Wigglesworth - JOY Unspeakable and Full of Glory

All they which are in Christ

All they which are in **Christ** will be caught up at His coming. The twenty-second chapter of Luke distinctly says that **Jesus** would not sit down again to break bread till the KINGDOM had come.

Now the KINGDOM is in every believer, and He will not sit down till every believer is there. The KINGDOM is in the believer, and the KINGDOM will come and millions and millions of people, I am sure, will be there who never received the **Holy Ghost**.

But they had the life of the **Christ** inside. When He comes Who is our life — it is not the **Holy Ghost** Who is the life; **Christ** is the life — when He comes Who is our life, then shall we go to the Life.

Humiliation & Humbleness

And so **God** would not have us under any circumstances to think that we are in the place of blessing when we are not in the place of humiliation and humbleness. It cannot be. **Jesus**, our blessed **Lord**, was the most meek, the most lovely, and the most beautiful in character.

You never find him like this: "Stand aside now. I am a man who has the gifts!" You never find that in **Jesus**, but he was so moved with COMPASSION that he could raise the widow's son. [Lk 7.11-17] We will not have had COMPASSION except by the inward power of **God** moving us. Everybody can be humble. It costs nothing except your pride and ugly self to be put out of the way.

Now what is a miracle? It is where the power of the **Spirit** of **God** comes to absolute helplessness, where no human aid can reach, but where **God** alone comes and performs the supernatural; when **God** comes and the body is made whole in a minute—not in an hour or a week, but in a minute—that is a miracle.

All COMPASSION is in the Heart.

As the **Lord Jesus** injected this **Wonderful** word, "Have faith in **God**," into the disciples, He began to show how it was to be. Looking around about Him He saw the mountains, and He began to bring a practical application. A truth means nothing unless it moves us. We can have our minds filled a thousand times, but it must get into our hearts if there are to be any results. All inspiration is in the heart. All COMPASSION is in the heart.

Looking at the mountains He said, "Shall not doubt in his heart." That is the barometer. You know exactly where you are. The man knows when he prays. If his heart is right how it leaps. No man is any good for **God** and never makes progress in **God** who does not hate sin. You are never safe.

But there is a place in **God** where you can love righteousness and where you can hate iniquity till the Word of **God** is a light in your bosom, quickening every fiber of your body, thrilling your whole nature. The pure in heart see **God**. Believe in the heart! What a word! If I believe in my heart **God** says I can begin to speak, and "whatsoever" I say shall come to pass.

If we preachers lose our COMPASSION we better stop preaching, for our preaching won't be any good. You will only be successful as a preacher as you let your heart become filled with the COMPASSION of Jesus.

Smith Wigglesworth - JOY Unspeakable and Full of Glory

Stephen cried out, "**Lord,** lay not this sin to their charge." As he was full of the **Spirit** he was full of love, and he manifested the very same COMPASSION for his enemies that **Jesus** did at Calvary. This being filled with the **Holy Ghost** means much in every way. It means constant filling, quickening, and a new life continually. Oh, it's lovely! We have a **Wonderful** gospel and a great Savior! If you will but be filled with the **Holy Ghost** you will have a constant spring within, yea, as your faith centers in the **Lord Jesus,** from within you shall flow rivers of living water.

If I Dare Believe

There is healing through the blood of **Christ** and deliverance for every captive. **God** never intended His children to live in misery because of some affliction that comes directly from the devil. A perfect atonement was made at Calvary. I believe that **Jesus** bore my sins, and I am free from them all. I am justified from all things if I dare believe. He Himself took our infirmities and bare our sicknesses; and if I dare believe, I can be healed.

See this poor, helpless man at the pool. "Wilt thou be made whole?" But there is a difficulty in the way. The man has one eye on the pool and one on **Jesus**. There are many people getting cross-eyed this way these days; they have one eye on the doctor and one on **Jesus**. If you will only look to **Christ** and put both your eyes on Him you can be made every whit whole, **Spirit,** soul and body. It is the word of the living **God** that they that believe should be justified, made free from all things. And whom the Son sets free is free indeed.

You say, "Oh, if I only could believe!" He understands. **Jesus** knew he had been a long time in that case. He is full of COMPASSION. He knows that kidney trouble, He knows those corns, He knows that neuralgia. There is nothing He does not know. He only wants a chance to show Himself merciful and gracious to you. But He wants to encourage you to believe Him.

If thou canst only believe, thou canst be saved and healed. Dare to believe that **Jesus** was wounded for your transgressions, was bruised for your iniquities, was chastised that you might have peace, and that by His stripes there is healing for you right here and now. You have failed because you have not believed Him. Cry out to Him even now, "**Lord**, I believe, help Thou mine unbelief."

These things are hidden and kept back from the wise and prudent, but the little children, the lowly ones, are the ones that receive. We cannot have faith if we have honor one of another. A man who is going on with **God** won't accept honor from his fellow beings.

God honors the man of a broken, contrite **Spirit**. How shall I get there? So many people want to do great things, and to be seen doing them, but the one that **God** will use is the one that is willing to be hidden. My **Lord Jesus** never said He could do things, but He did them.

When that funeral procession was coming up from Nain with the widow's son carried upon the bier, He made them lay it down. He spoke the word, "Arise!" and gave the son back to the widow. He had COMPASSION for her.

You and I will never do anything except in the place of COMPASSION. We shall never be able to remove cancer until we are immersed so deeply into the power of the Holy Ghost, that the COMPASSION of Christ is moving through us.

Smith Wigglesworth - JOY Unspeakable and Full of Glory

When I speak about the "fleshly tables of the heart," I mean the inward love. Nothing is so sweet to me as to know that the heart yearns with COMPASSION. Eyes may see, ears may hear, but you may be immovable on those two lines without you have an inward cry where "deep calleth unto deep."

When **God** gets into the depths of our hearts, He purifies every intention of the thoughts and the joys. We are told in the Word it is **JOY** unspeakable and full of glory.

TONGUES AND INTERPRETATION: "The **Spirit**, He Himself, it is He, that waketh thee morning by morning and unfolds unto thee in thy heart, tenderness, COMPASSION and love towards thy Maker till thou dost weep before Him and say to Him, in the **Spirit**, 'Thou art mine! Thou art mine!'"

Yes, He is mine! Beloved, He is mine!

"And such trust have we through **Christ** to **God**-ward:

"Not that we are sufficient of ourselves to think any thing as of ourselves; but our sufficiency is of **God**." (vv. 4, 5).

How to Live in the Miraculous!

This is a quick explanation of how to live and move in the realm of the miraculous. Seeing divine interventions of **God** is not something that just spontaneously happens because you have been born-again. There are certain biblical principles and truths that must be evident in your life. This is a very basic list of some of these truths and laws:

1. You must give **Jesus Christ** your whole heart. You cannot be lackadaisical in this endeavour. Being lukewarm in your walk with **God** is repulsive to the **Lord**. He wants 100% commitment. **Jesus** gave His all, now it is our turn to give our all. He loved us 100%. Now we must love Him 100%.

My son, give me thine heart, and let thine eyes observe my ways (Proverbs 23:26).

So then because thou art lukewarm, and neither cold nor hot, I will spew thee out of my mouth (Revelation 3:16).

2. There must be a complete agreement with **God**'s Word. We must be in harmony with the **Lord** in our attitude, actions, thoughts, and deeds. Whatever the Word of **God** declares in the New Testament is what we wholeheartedly agree with.

Can two walk together, except they be agreed? (Amos 3:3).

For the eyes of the LORD run to and fro throughout the whole earth, to shew himself strong in the behalf of them whose heart is perfect toward him (2 Chronicles 16:9).

3. Obey and do the Word from the heart, from the simplest to the most complicated request or command. No matter what the Word says to do, do it! Here are some simple examples: Lift your hands in praise, in everything give thanks, forgive instantly, gather together with the saints, and give offerings to the **Lord**, and so on.

I can of mine own self do nothing: as I hear, I judge: and my

Smith Wigglesworth - JOY Unspeakable and Full of Glory

judgment is just; because I seek not mine own will, but the will of the Father which hath sent me (John 5:30).

4. Make **Jesus** the highest priority of your life. Everything you do, do not do it as unto men, but do it as unto **God**.

If ye then be risen with Christ, seek those things which are above, where Christ sitteth on the right hand of God. Set your affection on things above, not on things on the earth (Colossians 3:1-2).

5. Die to self! The old man says, "My will be done!" The new man says, "**God**'s will be done!"

I am crucified with Christ: nevertheless I live; yet not I, but Christ liveth in me: and the life which I now live in the flesh I live by the faith of the Son of God, who loved me, and gave himself for me (Galatians 2:20).

Now if we be dead with Christ, we believe that we shall also live with him (Romans 6:8).

6. Repent the minute you get out of **God**'s will—no matter how minor, or small the sin may seem.

Revelation 3:19 As many as I love, I rebuke and chasten: be zealous therefore, and repent.

7. Take one step at a time. **God** will test you (not to do evil) to see if you will obey him. *Whatever He tells you to do: by His Word, by His **Spirit**, or within your conscience, do it.* He will never tell you to do something contrary to His nature or His Word!

For whosoever shall do the will of my Father which is in heaven, the same is my brother, and sister, and mother (Matthew 12:50).

ABOUT THE AUTHOR

Michael met and married his Wonderful wife (Kathleen) in 1978. As a direct result of the Author and his wife's personal, amazing experiences with God, they have had the privilege to serve as pastors/apostles, missionaries, evangelist, broadcasters, and authors for over four decades. By Gods Divine enablement's and Grace, Doc Yeager has written over 175 books, ministered over 10,000 Sermons, and having helped to start over 25 churches. His books are filled with hundreds of their amazing testimonies of Gods protection, provision, healing's, miracles, and answered prayers. They flow in the gifts of the Holy Spirit, teaching the word of God, Wonderful signs following and confirming God's word. Websites Connected to Doc Yeager.

www.docyeager.com

www.jilmi.org

www.wbntv.org

Some of the Books Written by Doc Yeager:

"Living in the Realm of the Miraculous – "1 to 5"
"I need God Cause I'm Stupid"
"The Miracles of Smith Wigglesworth"
"How Faith Comes 28 WAYS"

Smith Wigglesworth - JOY Unspeakable and Full of Glory

"Horrors of Hell, Splendors of Heaven"
"The Coming Great Awakening"
"Sinners in The Hands of an Angry GOD",
"Brain Parasite Epidemic"
"My JOURNEY to HELL" - illustrated for teenagers
"Divine Revelation of Jesus Christ"
"My Daily Meditations"
"Holy Bible of JESUS CHRIST"
"War In The Heavenlies - (Chronicles of Micah)"
"My Legal Rights to Witness"
"Why We (MUST) Gather! - 30 Biblical Reasons"
"My Incredible, Supernatural, Divine Experiences"
"How GOD Leads & Guides! - 20 Ways"
"Weapons of Our Warfare"
"How You Can Be Healed"
"Hell Is For Real"
"Heaven Is For Real"
"God Still Heals"
"God Still Provides"
"God Still Protects"
"God Still Gives Dreams & Visions"
"God Still Does Miracles"
"God Still Gives Prophetic Words"
"Life Changing Quotes of Smith Wigglesworth"

Made in the USA
Las Vegas, NV
11 February 2023

67331274R00115